The Non-Architect's Guide to Major Capital Projects: Planning, Designing, and Delivering New Buildings

By
Phillip S. Waite
Washington State University

Published by the
Society for College and University Planning
(SCUP)

Society for College and University Planning
339 E. Liberty Street, Suite 300
Ann Arbor, Michigan 48104
Phone: 734.998.7832
Fax: 734.998.6532
Web: www.scup.org

Printed in the United States of America

ISBN 0-9700413-7-3 original printing

ISBN 978-1-937724-59-7 print-on-demand 2018

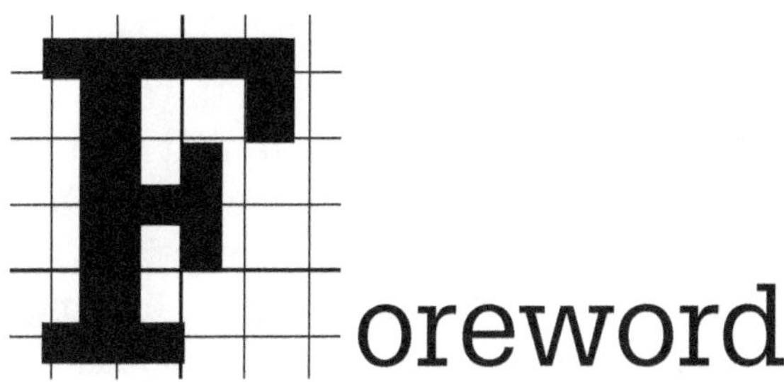

Foreword

"When we mean to build, We first survey the plot, then draw the model; And when we see the figure of the house, Then must we rate the cost of the erection, Which if we find outweighs ability, What do we then but draw anew the model. In fewer offices, or at least desist to build at all?"

—William Shakespeare, Henry IV, Part II
(Lord Bardolph to Hastings)

Planning in the time of Shakespeare seems to have been much like it is today: survey, draw, see if you can afford it. But the decisions to build "fewer offices" or, worse yet, "desist to build at all" can be very costly, especially if they come late in the planning process after considerable resources have been directed to a project.

In *The Non-Architect's Guide to Major Capital Projects*, Phil Waite provides a rewrite of Shakespeare with a useful, detailed, step-by-step guide to unpacking the process. His book can accompany the reader and prevent the loss of time and money as well as increase the chances of having a functional and successful building.

Phil Waite and I worked on several major capital projects together. He knows about buildings and he knows how to work with the users of those buildings and how to work with the architects of the buildings to realize optimum results. Phil taught me that I couldn't just sit back and let the architect try to read my mind; he taught me that planning a new building isn't something the architect or the users of the building should do alone; he taught me that the process of users and architects working together to put in place a useful, well-designed facility is both complex and exciting.

Phil focuses on the importance of a partnership between users and architect. His book holds the key to open dialog by providing a methodology to follow that is clear, precise, and simple. He shows readers what to do, just as he showed me in person when we worked together. He points out what could hold us back, and demonstrates how to proceed in ways that result in a building with usable space. The outcome is learning and knowing a process that will serve for any building.

Through his thoughtful explanations, Phil passes on to readers the excitement of being an integral part of the building process. By providing understanding of the terms and language of the process, he enables us to connect with others and make valuable contributions.

I am proud to have had Phil as a partner in several complex building processes and to call him a friend. I know his book will be a useful and positive contribution. *The Non-Architect's Guide to Major Capital Projects* will help only when you act on what you have learned. Don't just read Phil's work; make it your companion throughout a building process. Take his insight, knowledge, and the process he lays out, and act on it. His book can be the first step in achieving the building you want and deserve.

Dene Thomas
President, Lewis-Clark State College

Acknowledgements

We are all the sum of our training and experiences. To that end, I owe a debt of gratitude to Joanne Reece, assistant vice president for facilities (retired) at the University of Idaho, for the patience and years of training in capital planning she gave me.

My thanks to Bob Sena of Moore Iacofano Goltsman Inc. of Berkely, CA for what he has taught me about planning and for his helpful suggestions on an early draft of this work.

Special thanks go to Terry Calhoun, Sunny Beach, and Marc Johns at the Society for College and University Planning for their support and assistance, as well as a special acknowledgement to Kathy Benton at SCUP who suggested this book so many years ago—this was all your fault!

Thank you as well to all the consultants, contractors, and colleagues in higher education who took the time to answer my questions and gave me permission to quote them in the work.

Finally, a thank-you to my wife and children for their support, encouragement, and patience.

Phillip S. Waite

FROM THE PUBLISHER

The society is pleased to provide you with this useful resource on planning capital projects for a postsecondary environment. It is intended for people who are not architects or even planners but who have been asked to manage (or play an important role in) a major renovation or new construction project on campus.

Phil Waite's workshops and presentations for SCUP on this and similar topics have been well-received, and we are certain that the wisdom Phil packs into this book will create a positive effect on campuses all around the world.

The greatest positive effect from this book will come as a result of sharing the information by putting it in the hands of an entire planning committee or team so that the expertise and the common language can be utilized early on in the planning and design stages of a project.

Finally, the concept of environmental sustainability, which is addressed in this book, is nowhere more important than on college campuses, where the future leaders and professionals of tomorrow's society are being educated. There are many opportunities for readers of this book and others to champion the incorporation of money- and resource-saving ideas into capital projects at the pre-design and design stages. SCUP urges everyone in higher education to safeguard the world's environmental future whenever possible.

Thank you for purchasing this book. We wish all your campus projects great success.

Sincerely,

Jolene L. Knapp, CAE
SCUP Executive Director

L. Carole Wharton
SCUP 2004–2005 President

able of Contents

List of Figures

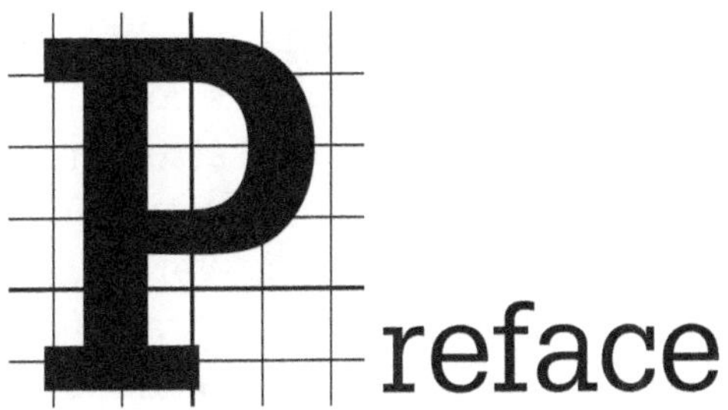

Preface

"Res quanto est mairo tanto est insidiosior."
("The bigger the undertaking, the trickier it is.")

– Syrus, Maxims

Planning, designing, and building a major capital project[1] is a long, complex, and often arduous process. It is difficult enough for architects and builders to manage, let alone for non-architects to understand. But non-architects are often placed in positions of leadership or responsibility in a capital project process. Administrators, managers, and academics, while no doubt experts within their own specialties, often have little or no training to prepare them for a role in a major capital project. The purpose of this book is to provide the non-architect with a broad framework of understanding in the steps, phases, and sequence of planning, designing, and delivering a capital project. It will familiarize the reader with the architectural and construction terminology used in planning and delivering a project. It will equip non-architects with sufficient background about each stage of the process to enable them to fulfill a role of influence in the delivery of a major capital project. It is a primer, not an encyclopedia. Although the text is addressed to those in higher education from the perspective of a colleague, the process it describes is the same for K–12 education, in the corporate world, or in the civic and municipal environment.

Pre-Design is the part of the project where non-architects are the most involved.

In a 1924 address to the English Architectural Association, Winston Churchill said, "There is no doubt whatever about the influence of architecture and structure upon human character and action. We make our buildings and afterwards they make us. They regulate the course of our lives." Nineteen years later, speaking to Parliament, he rephrased his oft-quoted statement this way: "We shape our buildings, and afterwards our buildings shape us."[2] While not a believer in architectural determinism, I do believe that our environment, especially the built environment within which we live and work, has a tremendous influence on the success of our endeavors. That being the case, architecture is too important to be left to architects alone. That's why you're involved in the process. You have important information, valuable insights, and worthwhile priorities that must be brought to bear on the process of shaping architecture. Even though you may not be an architect, you can exercise leadership in the capital project process because leadership is, at its root, influence.

The capital project process may seem baffling and even overwhelming. Nevertheless, there are few things more satisfying or pleasurable than seeing a major project successfully completed and knowing you positively influenced the outcome. Regardless of whether your project is a new high school, a university classroom or laboratory building, or a new office complex or manufacturing facility, you can have that effect when you know the basics of the process.

There are six stages of the project delivery process: (See Figure 1)

1) Planning or Pre-Design
2) Schematic Design
3) Design Development
4) Construction Documents

5) Construction Administration
6) Occupancy

These stages are not mutually exclusive and share some characteristics.[3] Each stage occupies a range on a continuum that has words and ideas on one end and built reality on the other.

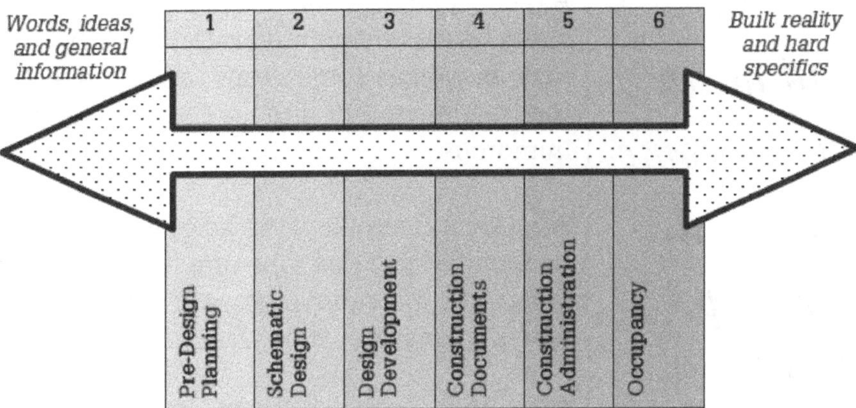

Figure 1. The Six Stages of a Project

Movement through each step on the continuum is from general information toward greater specificity. Each phase of the process has its own peculiarities and intricacies, bringing new levels of precision to the knowledge and information about the project. Each stage has its cast of players, although the role of institutional representative remains consistent throughout. This book will lead you through this sequence. The first chapter deals with the Pre-Design stage (stage 1); the second with the Design stages of the project (stages 2–4), and the third with Construction Administration and Construction Delivery (stages 5–6). The content of the book is deliberately weighted on the Pre-Design end of the project, for this is where non-architects are the most involved. Once the project moves past Pre-Design, its main weight rests on others.

I am deeply grateful to the consultants, contractors, and my colleagues in higher education who have graciously contributed

" 'Begin at the beginning,' the King said, gravely, 'and go on till you come to the end: then stop.' "

—Lewis Carroll

their thoughts and experiences to this work. You will find their contributions both integrated into the text and pulled out in large boxed quotations. Some boxes contain relevant quotations from other sources.

A glossary at the end of the book contains many terms and acronyms found in the text, as well as some terms not in the text that readers might find useful, or at least humorous.

Appendix A explains the language used by architects to describe graphics, and illustrates the various types of drawing views: plans, elevations, sections, etc.

For those interested in educating themselves further, in the area of capital projects specifically or architecture in general, an annotated bibliography is provided in the Appendix B.

Appendix C is a listing of consultant "Basic Services," as defined by the American Institute of Architects (AIA).

Chapter 1
The Pre-Design Planning Process

INTRODUCTION

The most important stage of any project is the first: **Pre-Design**, also called **Pre-Design Planning**.[4] It sets the stage for all that follows. Once a project has been approved, there is always a temptation to rush through the planning process to get to the more "glamorous" aspect of designing the facility. This is a serious mistake. Errors, omissions, and oversights in the pre-design / planning phase tend to become embedded in the design, and the consequences ripple across the life of the facility, often plaguing its users for years. Planning and programming can take as little as seven weeks or as long as 18 months. But when one considers that a campus facility may be used for a century or more, the time spent on planning provides a disproportionately large return on the investment.

It is at this stage of the project that you have the greatest opportunity for input into the process and impact on the final outcome. Your opportunity for input decreases as the project progresses. (See Figure 2)

The institution or agency that conceives and initiates a capital project should normally accomplish most of the steps in Pre-Design before they consider engaging a design consultant; it's simply too early in the process for that. Architects and engineers

To the carpenter whose only tool is a hammer, all problems look like nails.

are energetic, creative problem-solvers who are really good at what they do. But until your institution has worked through some of the steps of Pre-Design, you don't know if your problem is really a design problem or some other kind of problem. There are architects who tend to see all problems as design problems, even when they are actually management or organizational problems. A management or organizational problem can often be solved internally by a policy decision rather than a design, thus saving a lot of time and money.

Steps in the Pre-Design Planning process include:

- Establishing a planning committee.
- Defining the problem and identifying project origination.
- Defining the exact need that is to be met by this project.

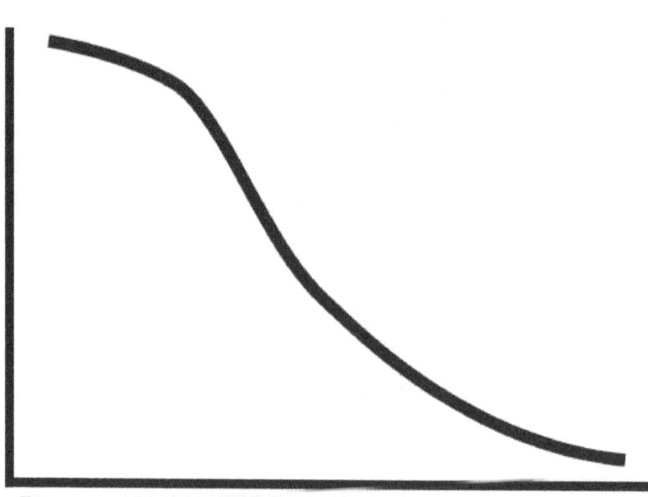

Figure 2. Ability to Influence Project Outcomes.

Source: Edward Adelman, AIA, Director of Capital Projects, Massachusetts State College Building Authority

- Establishing the parameters of that need.
- Coordinating the project with institutional policy.
- Creating a project program, a project budget, and a project schedule.

> *"Long-range planning does not deal with future decisions, but with the future of present decisions."*
>
> —Peter Drucker

ESTABLISHING THE PROJECT PLANNING COMMITTEE

In every institution, school, or business, someone (or some office) has the responsibility for planning and facilities development. At some point in the planning phase of a project, a "project planning committee"—or "planning task force" or "building committee"—should be established. Regardless of its name, its purpose is to help the person or office responsible for developing the project. The structure of this committee will vary from institution to institution and from project to project. If the institution or school system is large enough, a staff architect or planner may be tasked with leading this committee. More often than not, however, the titular head will be someone from the administration or the faculty (hence the need for this book!), with an institution's in-house architect simply providing expertise and guidance as a committee member.

Who should be on the planning committee? Project "stakeholders"—representatives of the programs, departments, or units that will use the new facility—usually form the key membership. Other members might include someone familiar with the institution's capital outlay process, someone from the facilities management or physical plant office, someone representing institutional fundraising and development, student representatives, and someone representing institutional administration. Some committee members may represent multiple constituen-

. . . at least one "opponent" of the project should be on the committee as well. The role of critic and devil's advocate provides a check to the often unbridled enthusiasm of a project's proponents . . .

cies. I believe that at least one "opponent" of the project should be on the committee as well. The role of critic and devil's advocate provides a check to the often unbridled enthusiasm of a project's proponents. Further, it's usually better to co-opt the opposition by including them up front in the process rather than having them sniping from the sidelines.

How many members should a committee have? In my experience, five to seven people aren't enough and 14 to 15 are too many. A membership of nine to 12 is manageable and insures a sufficiently diverse representation. With a smaller group, you run the risk of insufficient input and a perceived disenfranchisement of the user groups, while a larger group can fall prey to information overload, not to mention the difficulty of coordinating the schedules of more than a dozen people.

Next, it is vital to establish the charge of the committee and clearly define the role it will play. Some committees are established to provide input and play an advisory role to the consultant and to the planning process, but have no decision-making authority. Other committees are charged with input, review, and decision-making. It's important to distinguish between the authority to make decisions and the authority to advise the decision-makers. Many planning committees become discouraged and feel disenfranchised when they find they are simply being asked for advice when they assumed they had a policy and decision-making role. Much angst can be prevented if the exact structure, role, and responsibilities of the committee are defined at its first meeting.

The first task of the planning committee in Pre-Design should be the formulation of the "problem statement," which defines exactly what the problem is and why a proposed building project is the best solution.[5] The problem definition should start with determining the project's *originating source*, i.e. the driving force or motivation behind it, because how a project originates often affects how it is delivered, its level of complexity, and related reporting requirements.

> *"With the possible exception of the equator, everything begins somewhere."*
>
> —Peter Robert Flemming

PROJECT ORIGINATION

The following are some possible sources of a major capital project:

- Strategic Initiatives
- Master Planning
- Aging Physical Plant
- Natural Disasters
- Federal Initiatives
- State / System Initiatives
- Private Donors
- Institutional or Program Growth

Strategic Initiatives

A project can originate from an institutional response to industry or societal needs or to competitive pressures. For example, an institution may develop a new facility, center, or institute for the highly specialized research program of a "star" faculty member. Businesses often respond strategically to competitive pressures with a new facility. A project that originates this way is likely to be expedited in order to respond in a timely manner to a strategic opportunity.

Master Planning

Just as a city is more than a collection of buildings, a campus is the integration of buildings, landscapes, roads, parking lots, and infrastructure. Every campus needs a master plan to guide its physical development, and all major capital projects should be implemented within the framework of that plan. No project, regardless of its source, should be conceived or developed as an independent island disconnected from the context of the campus.

Aging Physical Plant

"Between 1950 and 1975, higher education's physical space tripled in size. More college and university space was constructed during this 25-year period than in the prior 200 years."[6] The average age of the buildings on the campus where I worked was 39 years, and this is close to the national average. Even if you never have a capital project resulting from a strategic initiative, sooner or later you will have one resulting from the need to replace aging facilities. The cost of deferred maintenance on campuses across the country exceeds $26 billion and growing yearly. These buildings need to be replaced, renovated, and remodeled. K–12 schools are in the same situation.

Natural Disasters

Earthquakes, hurricanes, floods, and even volcanoes can be the originating sources for projects. Campuses in California have been especially hard hit in the last two decades, with earthquake damage necessitating hundreds of millions of dollars in renovations and new construction. Hurricanes in the southeastern U.S. and tornadoes in the Midwest have spurred similar expenditures. The difficulty in planning a project under these conditions is that there are usually multiple initiatives under way at the same time. Time and energy are consumed by crisis management, and planning for the future is rushed in an effort to get "back to normal" as soon as possible.

Federal Initiatives

These can be in any number of areas—space research, food research, transportation research, military and defense, etc. Institutional strategic initiatives are often tied to federal programs; it's amazing how the availability of federal money can turn a low priority into a high one. The issues here are mainly timing and reporting. Coordinating with federal budget cycles is always a challenge. Federal dollars often have a deadline by which all dollars have to be either expended or committed, i.e. a bid let or contract signed even though construction has not begun. Extensions are easy to come by with some agencies. With others, money that is not spent reverts to the government.

Further, reporting requirements differ between agencies. Some give you the money and ask you to report back to them when all is said and done. Others require bi-monthly reporting and approval of every payment made to a consultant or contractor. Make sure you have an institutional representative with both the responsibility and authority to deal with the reporting requirements.

State / System Initiatives

Your institution may be part of a state school or education system that introduces, for example, a system-wide technology-learning requirement. If it isn't an unfunded mandate, you may actually receive dollars to remodel an old facility or build a new one. These are very much like Strategic Initiatives, except they are imposed from without, rather than originating within the institution. Again, reporting standards and requirements for this kind of project will differ from an internally or federally funded one.

Private Donors

While not often involved in commercial initiatives or public schools, private donors are often pursued in higher education. Sometimes the donor has no interest in your master plan or strategic initiatives but wants to build a building or fund a program that isn't even on your planning "radar screen." While it is important

The **Strategic Plan** *tells you* **when** *to build it. The* **Academic Plan** *tells you* **what** *to include in the program. The role of the* **Master Plan** *is to tell you* **where** *to build your project.*

never to look a gift horse in the mouth, don't be deluded into thinking these are easy projects or that there are not strings attached to the money. Although it distorts the meaning of the word "gift", many institutions simply are not in a position to reject such donations. It is a rare institutional administration that has the integrity to turn down money rather than compromise its pre-existing master or strategic plan. As with other funding sources described above, reporting requirements vary among donors. It's important that the fundraising and development side of the institution is in accord with the administration on seeking donations that align with both the institutional strategic plan and the campus master plan.

Institutional or Program Growth
Sometimes a project may have nothing to do with the federal or state government, a strategic initiative, or a natural disaster. It may be necessitated by the normal growth of an institution or a specific program that has outgrown its space. The old space may not even be outdated, just not large enough.

COORDINATING POLICY WITH PHYSICAL DEVELOPMENT

One of the principle purposes of the Pre-Design phase is ensuring that the capital project advances in coordination with the policies, directions, vision, mission, and strategic plan of the institution. This may sound obvious, but all too often a project comes along that is completely disconnected from an institution's strategic plan, academic plan, or physical development master plan. How does this happen? At some institutions, individual faculty are allowed and encouraged to pursue whatever grant funding is available. Sometimes grants are awarded that obligate an institution to provide matching funds or in-kind donations (like facility renovations). Regardless of how good the project may be for the individual department or researcher, in the absence of some coordinating structure, such situations often find the institution scrambling to find matching funds. Thus, a grant-funded project may leap to the top of the institution's project priority list, ahead of projects that may actually respond to a greater institutional need. A large private donation to a specific program, department or college within the university can have the same effect. Either way, a capital project which may or may not align with pre-existing policies, directions and plans is "sprung" on the institution. Part of the planning committee's responsibility is to ensure that the pre-design effort for the proposed project takes into account the institution's strategic plan, academic plan, and campus master plan. The strategic plan will tell you both what and when to build, the academic plan will tell you what to include in the program, and the master plan will tell you where to build your project and what it should look like.

ESTABLISHING THE NEED / OPPORTUNITY

After determining the proposed capital project's origination and ensuring that the project is coordinated with institutional plans and policies, the next step is to define the needs that the project is meeting, as well as their extent. The means to do this include:

- Feasibility Studies
- Facility Studies
- Benchmarking
- Programming

Feasibility Study

The "objective of a feasibility study is to determine if a proposed building project is financially, physically, and legally possible."[7] Though often provided by an architect or other consultants, a feasibility study can (and I think should) be performed by institutional staff. In addition to a financial and legal review, it can also include space planning, development, and marketing.

A feasibility study may also tell you if the project is really necessary. It should try to determine if there is an alternative way of organizing, operating, and interacting that can advance the mission of the institution without having to build a new building. At one institution, for instance, one department within a college loudly insisted that it needed its own building. The institutional planning office performed a feasibility study that included a look at the department's space utilization. The planners came to the (unpopular) conclusion that not only did the department not need any new space but, when benchmarked against national averages, it had more than it could effectively use. The planners actually proposed reassigning some of its space to other departments within the college. (This may explain why planners are often vilified on campus!)

Facility Study

A facility study is a basically a feasibility study dealing specifically with the facility options for meeting an institutional need. It can include an inventory of existing facilities, utilization rates, estimates of space needs, and an evaluation of the quality of existing space. An analysis of alternative siting options may also be included.

Although usually performed under contract by an architectural or planning firm, a large-enough institution may have facility planning or management staff that are specifically tasked with performing this kind of study.

Benchmarking

A good feasibility study or programming exercise will include benchmarking. Benchmarking is an ongoing, systematic methodology for identifying, measuring, and comparing a facility's size, use, quality and quantity of space, and costs with those of peer institutions or agencies. For example, if other schools use a standard of 150 square feet per faculty office, and you find that most of your faculty offices are 95 square feet, you've just benchmarked a critical component of faculty recruitment and retention. Why would new faculty want to come to your institution when another has better facilities? Using benchmarking this way establishes the need for new space based on nationally recognized standards, rather than easily dismissed in-house preferences.

Another critical component of benchmarking is space utilization and management. Suppose that your campus has one million net assignable square feet of facility space. If, through benchmarking and effective, targeted space management, you could increase your space utilization rate by just 5 percent, what have you gained? Nearly 50,000 net square feet! That's 50,000 square feet that you don't have to build new. If we assume that the new space is going to cost $250 per square foot, not building 50,000 new square feet is a savings of over $12.5 million! It may not be exactly the kind of space you need, and it may not be exactly where you want it. But at the very least, it might reduce the amount of new space you have to build. In this era of scarce resources, a savings of that size is worth the effort of benchmarking and space management.

Programming

Programming is the heart of the pre-design stage and one of the central responsibilities of the planning committee. The primary idea behind architectural programming is "the search for sufficient information to clarify, to understand, and to state the problem."[8] "Programming is a systematic method of inquiry that delineates the context within which the designing must be done as well as defines the requirements that a successful project must meet."[9] A full architectural program is a written document that includes an articulation of the specific space requirements to meet the functional and program needs of the proposed project.

If the institution does not have the internal staff to direct or carry out this effort, a planner or architect who specializes in programming is often hired to work with the planning committee to develop the program. Hiring a planner or architect to work with the planning committee on programming does not obligate the institution to use the same consultant to design the project. In fact, the consultant doing the programming is frequently not the consultant who designs the project. This is because programming and designing are fundamentally different processes that require different mental activities. Programming is an objective process of, in essence, problem-seeking: gathering, sorting, and categorizing information, as well as evaluating it to determine what is important and what is irrelevant. It requires a certain skill in abstract thinking. On the other hand, designing is a subjective process of problem-solving. It requires competency with physical concepts, three-dimensional visualization, and a host of other subjective, intuitive skills. As the architect and author William Pena says, "These are two distinct processes, requiring different attitudes, even different capabilities. . . . The difference between programming and design is the difference between analysis and synthesis. In analysis, the parts of a design problem are separated and identified. In synthesis, the parts are put together to form a coherent design solution."[10] Programmers tend to be analytical, big-picture thinkers, problem-oriented, with a tendency to not rush to closure. Their tools are ideas and words. Designers tend to be less interested in the big picture and more in the details. They are synthetical, solution-oriented, and strive to arrive at closure. Their tools are images rather than words. Please realize that I've painted these differences with a broad brush and made sweeping generalizations. Although it is rare, a few professionals are competent at both kinds of mental processes. The point is not that one is right and the other wrong, but that it is important to find the right consultant at the right stage in the process, because a successful project uses the right process at the right time. (This is why I previously suggested that it is counter-productive to hire a designer too early in the pre-design stage.)

Are you a big-picture thinker, or more detail-oriented? It's not that one is good and the other bad. They're just different, and each is needed. Part of your role in this process is to understand the distinctions between these two processes, where you best fit, and how you can help both programming and designing to be successful.

THE PRODUCTS OF PROGRAMMING

A good pre-design report will include all the negotiations, decisions, compromises, trade-offs, and results of the pre-design stage. In addition to the feasibility study, it will provide an architectural program, a project budget, and a project schedule. As I stated above, a full architectural program is "a written document that includes an articulation of the specific space requirements to meet the functional and program needs of the proposed project." It often includes "room data sheets," detailed written descriptions of each space or room in the proposed facility, usually accompanied by a drawing or diagram that illustrates critical physical and spatial relationships. While these diagrams and drawings should not be construed as design documents—the actual final design is unlikely to look at all like the diagrams in the program—a successful design will capture the functional and spatial relationships thus illustrated.

The total of all the space requirements listed in the program is called the Net Assignable Square Feet (NASF or NSF) needed to solve the problem.

Understanding Gross Vs. Net Square Feet

This can be a confusing concept for non-architects or those not involved in space management, but understanding the difference

. . . understanding the difference between gross square feet and net square feet is critical.

between gross square feet and net square feet is critical. Here are the definitions:

Gross Square Feet (GSF): "All of the floor space inside a building measured from the outside surfaces of exterior walls."[11] The gross is all of the building that you have to build, including parts that can't be assigned for individual or department use, such as elevators, stairwells, restrooms, hallways, atria, and the floor area under interior walls. (See Figure 3.)

Net Assignable Square Feet (NASF): "The net floor space in a building measured from the inside surfaces of exterior walls and excluding interior walls and partitions, mechanical equipment rooms, lavatories, janitorial closets, elevators, stairways, major circulation corridors, aisles, and elevator lobbies."[12] In essence, it's those specific floor areas of the building that can assigned to an individual program, department, or user. (See Figure 3.)

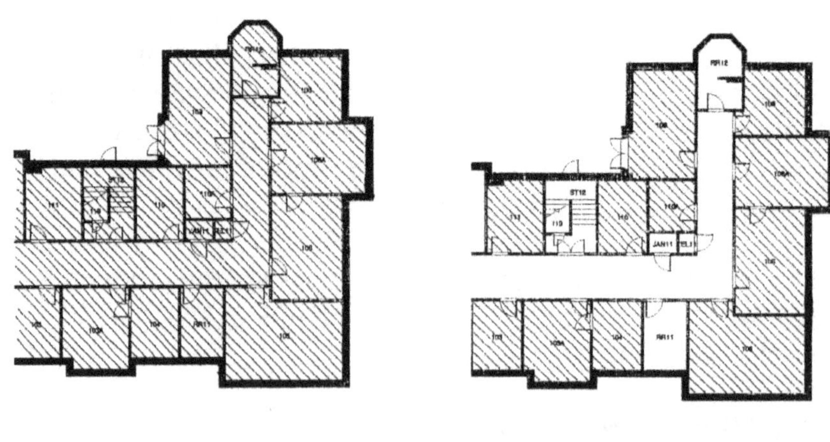

Gross Square Feet — **Net Square Feet**

Figure 3. Plan of gross vs. net square feet

Building Efficiency Ratio

The "Building Efficiency Ratio" is the percentage of a building that can actually be assigned for use. The figure for most buildings is between 55 percent and 65 percent.

Obviously, different building types have different degrees of efficiency. Buildings that have large open areas are highly efficient, since relatively little space is taken up by interior walls or separate corridors. Gyms, recreation centers, and physical education buildings can have an efficiency ratio as high as 75 percent, while laboratories have a much lower ratio due to the amount of space used for mechanical systems and utility infrastructure. A "wet" research laboratory can have a building efficiency ratio as low as 50 percent. (see chart at right) A low efficiency ratio doesn't necessarily mean a building is poorly laid out or inefficiently designed. Student unions, for example, because they usually have wide corridors and informal gathering spaces distributed about the building, often have very low efficiency ratios.

Typical Building Efficiencies

Building Type	Efficiency
Office Building	55% – 65%
Classroom Buildings	60% – 70%
Teaching Labs	55% – 70%
Research Lab (Dry)	60% – 70%
Research Lab (Wet)	45% – 65%
Unions	55% – 65%
Libraries	60% – 70%
Physical Education	65% – 75%

Understanding the distinction between gross and net is the key to unlocking the rest of the Pre-Design data. The programming process will tell you how many net square feet are needed to

As a general rule of thumb, the building efficiency ratio for most buildings is between 55% and 65%.

meet the program goals. Dividing that number by the building efficiency ratio will tell you how many gross square feet are needed to meet the project goals. Knowing the gross square footage of your proposed facility allows you to calculate a construction budget, and knowing the construction budget allows you to calculate the project budget, which is the total amount of funding required—including owner's costs—to plan, design, and construct the facility.

At one campus that shall remain nameless, the director of student services was assigned to figure out the space needs for his new student services building and then put together the budget for it. He simply measured all the rooms and offices in the current building, added some space for functions that they wanted to offer, totaled the square footage and multiplied by $110 per square foot . . . because the contractor who built his house had told him that an expensive home could be built in their area for that price. He didn't take into account that his budget had to cover the gross square feet required, not just the net, nor that institutional buildings cost significantly more than the light-frame construction in a private residence. Not only was his proposed cost per square foot less than half of what it should have been, but he had also omitted 40 percent of the building. These simple errors meant that the budget assigned to his project was less than half of what was actually needed for it. This necessitated a return visit to the state legislature by the institution's vice president for finance to seek additional funding—not the kind of experience such an official looks forward to.

The Project Budget

The Project Budget is the sum of the Construction Budget and the Owner's Budget. It represents the total cost of building and occupying a new or renovated facility.

The Construction Budget covers new construction, the renovation of existing facilities, site work, utilities, and infrastructure. All other expenses related to the delivery of the project are in the Owner's Budget, including architectural and engineering consultant fees, land costs, owner costs, contingencies, and furnishings, fixtures, and equipment.

As a very general rule, and depending on the type of project, the Construction Budget is usually 60% to 80% of the Project Budget.

Just as 55 percent to 65 percent is a typical ratio of net to gross square feet, the Construction Budget is usually 60 percent to 80 percent of the Project Budget. That means that if your Project Budget is $10 million, your Construction Budget (which determines how many square feet can be built) should be between $6 and $8 million.

At one institution, a new facility was planned with a $10 million Construction Budget, but the president and other officials were telling everyone that $10 million was the Project Budget. The institution's development office promptly raised the money, only to discover that the amount really needed was closer to $16 million when all of the owner's costs were taken into account! In order to avoid these kinds of misunderstandings, it is crucial for everyone involved in a project—especially those who will speak from a position of authority—to understand the difference between the Project Budget and the Construction Budget.

The Owner's Budget

The Owner's Budget covers the project's non-construction expenses, such as:

- **Consultant Fees.** These are usually for architectural and engineering consultants, but can also include landscape architects, interior designers, signage experts, audio-visual designers, telecommunications experts, and acousticians.
- **Owner Costs.** Examples are land acquisition, demolition, soil tests, site survey, insurance, permits, moving and relocations, physical plant support, facility tours, utilities, and material testing.
- **Furnishings, Fixtures, and Equipment (FF&E).** These include blinds, carpet, shelves, casework, movable lighting, and other equipment that is not hard-wired or hard-plumbed into the building.
- **Contingencies.** These are necessary in the absence of exact information at particular times and to cover unforeseen conditions. The two types are a Construction Contingency, a percentage based on the Construction Budget, usually 5 percent on new construction and 10 percent on remodels, and a Project Contingency (also called an Owner's Contingency), usually 5 percent of the Project Budget. The Project Contingency should be reduced at each phase of the project.
- **Inflation** is usually calculated to the midpoint of construction. It is often included in the Construction Contingency

Let's explore each of these a little more.

Consultant Fees

There are several ways to arrive at a basic services fee (See Appendix C for a list of what the AIA considers "basic services") for architectural and engineering consultants:

1. A stipulated sum based on the architect's proposal. The architect or other consultant simply specifies a fee based on however they choose to calculate it.
2. A stipulated sum per unit on what is to be built. For example, if you are constructing new student apartments on campus, you may get a fee proposal based on "X" number of dollars per apartment unit designed and built.

3. A percentage of construction costs. Most states and institutions determine fees based on a percentage of the construction cost. The percentage varies depending on the size of the budget and the complexity of the project. A larger construction budget means a smaller percentage for the fee. A complex project warrants a higher percentage. The rule of thumb for a project of average size and complexity is that the basic services fee will equal 8 percent of the construction cost. Examples of a complex project would be a research laboratory or performing arts center. Average projects would be a classroom facility, gymnasium, office building, or recreation building. A simple project would be a warehouse, greenhouse, or service garage. For a complex project with a construction budget less than $500,000, the fee can approach 12 percent of the construction budget. For a simple project with a construction budget less than $500,000, a fee of 8 percent is appropriate. At the other end of the scale, standard fees are 6.5 percent for a complex project with a $30 million budget and 4.5 percent for a simple project with a comparable budget.

The rule of thumb for a project of average size and complexity is that the basic services fee will equal 8% of the construction cost

4. Hourly rates. These vary between firms and geographic regions, but it is not unusual for a firm principal to be billed out at around $200 per hour or more. Project architects will usually be billed at between half and three-quarters the rate of a principal.
5. Any combination of the above.

Regardless of how the fee is determined, consultants should never be selected on the basis of fees, but on the basis of their qualifications. Fees are dynamic and can be negotiated; qualifications are fairly constant.

Fee Distribution
The consultant fee package is distributed over the course of the entire project. A typical distribution (plus or minus 2 percent depending on the complexity and size of the project) is shown below.

Even though the total consultant fee for basic services is based on a percentage of the Construction Budget, the amount spent on programming is based on the total Project Budget.

Owner Costs
These can include:

- Land Acquisition. If the institution doesn't own the land where the proposed facility will stand, it must be acquired.
- Demolition of Existing Facilities.
- Site Surveys. A certified survey by a civil engineer is often the first step undertaken once a site is selected.
- Soil Tests. These indicate what kind of foundation and structural system will be required for the building, a significant issue to define early in the process. They also determine if hazardous waste is present that must be mitigated before construction can begin.

PHASE	**FEES**
Predesign / Programming	1%
Schematic Design	14%
Design Development	20%
Construction Documents	38%
Bidding	2%
Construction Administration	24%
Project Closeout	1%
TOTAL	100%

- Insurance.
- Facility Tours. When an institution is considering a new facility, especially of a type not currently on its campus, the building committee will often tour other institutions to see how they've addressed similar needs. It is not possible to

overstate the value of facility tours in providing a building committee with concrete examples both of what they want and what they don't want, but this is a cost that must be included in the Owner's Budget.

- Permits. Some institutions are not required to either secure local building permits or meet zoning requirements. Less fortunate institutions must meet all local ordinances governing construction of a new facility.
- Relocations and Interim Space. A mistake often made in pre-design planning is failure to budget for final move-in expenses, or for providing interim space for displaced departments and units. As Zelinda Zingaro, senior project manager at San Francisco State University, told me, "It is vital to have sufficient temporary space available to house programs and offices and labs when construction begins. This is an expensive undertaking but essential to maintaining ongoing academic programs and research."
- Physical Plant Support. There will always be a need for facilities management and/or physical plant support. This must also be budgeted for or the institution will be forced to make up this expense elsewhere.
- Utility Infrastructure. Most states define the boundary of a building project as five feet outside the wall. But what if a new facility requires additional power, water, steam, or chilling capacity? These utilities are always outside the five-foot limit. Bringing the institution's utility infrastructure to the building is an expense that must be borne by someone, somewhere. It is best to include all utility infrastructure costs in the owner's budget.
- Information and Telecommunications Infrastructure. Sometimes this is included in the utility infrastructure budget, but I recommend it be handled separately because of its importance to the overall mission of the institution.
- Sustainability Analysis. If the institution will be seeking LEED (Leadership in Energy and Environmental Design) certification for its facility, or at least making it "sustainable" in some form, a sustainability analysis needs to be performed very early in the project. Sustainability is not the kind of requirement that can be tacked on once a project is well underway. Like Commissioning or Construction Management (below), it must be incorporated right from the beginning.

- Building Commissioning Services. Commissioning will be discussed in Chapter 3, "Construction Administration," and is included here because it is clearly the owner's decision to use commissioning and thus it must be part of the owner's budget, and also because commissioning often begins in the Pre-Design stage of a project. It is an especially valuable service when developing a high-tech research or laboratory facility.
- Construction Management Services. These will also be discussed in Chapter 3, but the decision to engage construction management services should be considered in the Pre-Design stage. Although some believe that Pre-Design is too early to consider construction issues, it may actually be the best time for it. According to Simon F. Etzel, senior vice president, Konover Construction Corporation, Farmington, CT, "There is a tremendous benefit that we can offer our clients if we're brought in at the beginning of the design process. We can help keep the project on budget and ensure constructability by working collaboratively with the architect and the client at the very early stages of design, evaluating the design concepts and providing vital feedback on how the design will affect the budget, on whether there are constructability issues, and what alternatives the owner and architect might consider." His comments are echoed by Terry Krause, regional director of higher education for Turner Construction, New York, NY, who says clients should consider bringing the contractor on board very early "to get the benefits of the pre-construction process: value engineering, estimating, constructability issues, and safety and logistics planning."
- Third-Party Cost Estimating. While some states mandate that all projects employ a third-party cost estimator, many do not. However, it is an excellent idea if the Owner's Budget can bear the expense.
- Material Testing. This testing ensures the quality of construction materials and methodologies. It is sometimes included in the Construction Budget.
- Special Services. "Special services" or "additional services" are defined by the AIA and cover project efforts not included in "Basic Services." (See appendix C for the AIA's listing of basic and special services.)

Furnishings, Fixtures, and Equipment (also known as FF&E)
Furnishings, fixtures, and equipment are distinct from fixed equipment, which refers to those building elements that are hard-wired or hard-plumbed into the facility and could not be easily moved, or are essential to the building's operation. Examples of fixed equipment are elevators, plumbing fixtures, fume hoods, and heating, ventilation, and air conditioning equipment (HVAC). For planning purposes, fixed equipment can be calculated at 8 percent of the construction budget, which is where it is included in the vast majority of projects.[13]

FF&E generally refers to movable assets that are not affixed to any part of a room or building, such as furniture, as well as those pieces of furniture or equipment that are attached to the room or building but are not permanently affixed, or can be removed without costly alterations or repairs, or can be used after removal. Examples include shelving, coat racks, window coverings (blinds or drapes), artwork, rugs, etc. However, there are few elements of a project that can vary as much depending on building type as FF&E. Even the definition can change from state to state and from institution to institution. In some

Third-party estimating "provides an independent, non-adversarial body involved in the project. The third-party estimator can provide milestone estimates at each stage of a project. The advantage of starting early is that costs can be monitored and tracked throughout the design stages."

—James Vermeulen, Vermeulen Cost Consultants, Cambridge, Massachusetts instances, casework (cabinets) is included in the Construction Budget; in others, it's considered part of FF&E. Sometimes the distinction is based on the usable life of the piece. For instance, a finish flooring (like tile or seamless flooring) that has a life span of 20 or more years is considered fixed equipment and is included in the Construction Budget. But if the floor covering is a carpet, whose life span is only five to 10 years, then it falls within the FF&E category.

It's difficult to assign a dollar amount to furnishings, fixtures, and equipment in the Owner's Budget. The figure will be determined by the particular building type. A general rule of thumb is that an amount equal to at least 5 percent to 10 percent of the Construction Budget should be initially allocated for FF&E. The percentage should be higher for laboratories or other complex facilities.

> *The building type will determine how much of the Owner's Budget is allocated to FF&E. Very generally, at least an amount equal to 5% to 10% of the Construction Budget should be initially allocated to FF&E.*

Sometimes the FF&E budget is treated as a "contingency"—something to be purchased if enough funds remain at the end of the project, since the furniture and blinds and area rugs and shelving and artwork can be added late in the process or even after the building is occupied. Occupants can move in and use furniture from their previous locations. (There is nothing quite like a brand-spanking-new building with old beat-up furniture—but it happens!)

The chief lesson to be learned from this discussion is the importance of verifying exactly what is included in FF&E at your institution and making sure all building committee members and constituents know what is in FF&E and what is not. Everyone involved in the project must understand the difference between what's in the Construction Budget, i.e. fixed equipment, as opposed to what's in FF&E as part of the Owner's Budget. Invariably, some items aren't in either budget, and it's far better to know what they are up front rather than after the fact. Laboratory equipment is a good example; some pieces are hard-wired or hard-plumbed into the building, but are not considered fixed equipment and are too expensive to put in the FF&E budget. These often have to be secured through other means, such as departmental operations budgets or equipment grants.

(1) Project Contingency

- Owner's Contingency
- Design Contingency

(2) Construction Contingency

- New Construction
- Remodel Construction

Contingencies & Inflation

The purpose of a contingency is to protect everyone involved from the vagaries of the unknown conditions and requirements of a project, which are reduced as it goes forward and more accurate information is developed. As the number of unknowns decreases, contingency amounts can be released into the Construction Budget.

There are four types of contingencies that should be included in a Project Budget:

- The Project Contingency is usually 5 percent of the total Project Budget and is usually composed of an Owner's Contingency and a Design Contingency.
- The Owner's Contingency is the institution, agency, or owner's safety cushion, necessary because of the number of unknowns that can develop over the course of the project.
- The Design Contingency is usually controlled by the owner, sometimes by the consultant. It covers unknowns in the

design process or addresses additions to the project's scope that may develop in the course of design. Some owners keep the Design Contingency a secret in the belief that knowing the available contingency will encourage the architectural and engineering consultant to push for more fees by drawing out the design process. I have never known an architect to do that. I believe it is better to conduct the entire project in an open, honest, and transparent way for all parties.

- The Construction Contingency is usually included in the Construction Budget but is sometimes held separately by the owner as part of the Project Budget. The Construction Contingency is calculated not on the Project Budget, but rather on the Construction Budget. For new construction, and depending on the complexity of the project, 5 percent of the Construction Budget is standard. If the project involves remodeling, the Construction Contingency is often calculated at 10 percent of the Construction Budget. The age of the building being remodeled and whether the building has "historic building status" (H.B.S.) can drive up the contingency on a remodel. Remodel contingency on a building with H.B.S. can be as high as 20 percent of the Construction Budget. Another factor that affects contingencies on older buildings is the status and quality of record drawings, i.e. does the institution or owner have high quality "as-built drawings" of the building, including all construction or remodel work performed since its original construction? The presence of high-quality record drawings can reduce the remodel contingency, whereas the lack of such drawings can increase it.

Inflation

Depending on how long it takes to secure full project funding, inflation can be calculated on the entire Project Budget, or just the Construction Budget. On a large Construction Budget, inflation can take a serious toll if it is not planned for. Inflation is calculated on the Construction Budget to the midpoint of construction.

Establishing the Budget

How do all these pieces come together in creating a budget? Let's develop an example. We'll assume that your institution wants to build a new building for your College of Education that will include classrooms, faculty offices, a library and media resource area, and informal gathering and study spaces for students. We will also assume that the pre-design programming exercise has defined a need for 68,000 net square feet. Because of the mix of spaces, we will assume a building efficiency ratio of 65 percent. Dividing the net square feet needed by the efficiency ratio gives us the gross square feet required:

68,000 NSF ÷ .65 = 104,615 GSF.

Local building conditions and past experience tell you that the quality of facility that you want to build will cost approximately $250 per gross square foot.[14]

$250 per GSF x 104,615 GSF = $26,153,750

Using this figure of slightly more than $26 million, we can develop the rest of the proposed budget. Remember, the budget developed in the Pre-Design stage will have a margin of error of plus or minus 20 percent, due to all the unknowns that have yet to be fleshed out. As the process moves forward and more accurate information is developed, the budget can be fine-tuned with increasing accuracy until the final Construction Estimate is developed, which should be within plus or minus 2 percent of the maximum allowable construction cost (the MACC, see below).

Let's go through this budget line by line.

Line 1 – Building Costs. These are based on the gross square feet developed by the pre-design programming effort. The cost per square foot of $250 is probably low. More accurate square foot cost data can be found using a reference like the Means Cost

To the general public, a project isn't done until it looks done. It won't "look done" until the landscaping, parking, sidewalks, etc., are installed.

Estimating Guide, which surveys national data for many different building types.

Line 2 – Fixed Equipment. The fixed equipment is often lumped under Line 1. I've separated it to highlight the distinction between fixed equipment and furnishings, fixtures, and equipment.

Line 3 – Site Development. Site acquisition is not included in this number. Site development includes all the landscaping, access driveways, parking spaces, etc., required to make the facility useable. The cost of site development varies widely, depending on each project's site requirements. It is often lumped under "Building Costs," but I think that is a mistake. If it isn't included as a separate line item in the Pre-Design budget, it won't be added later. It is too easily overlooked and omitted from the project. Moreover, including it in the Construction Budget makes it too susceptible to being whittled away by the architect, who may not consider it a high priority. I admit that, as a licensed landscape architect, I may be biased here. But I've seen it happen too many times. The point is that few things are more likely to make a nice building look bad than placing it in a field of mud and gravel because the landscaping was left out, or cut out, of the budget. There is always the temptation to minimize or eliminate site development with the promise that it will be added later. The problem is that "later" doesn't always come. The appearance of an unfinished project can plague a campus for years. It isn't just an embarrassment to the architect. It reflects on the administration, the facility users, and the entire institution.

Line 4 – Construction Budget. The Construction Budget is the total of the first three line items: Building Costs, Fixed Equipment, and Site Development. Many of the rest of the line items in the budget are based on this subtotal. Some states and institutions call this number the maximum allowable construction cost, or the MACC. It forms the basis for many budget decisions that follow.

> *Maximum allowable construction cost, or the MACC*

Line 5 – Inflation. Normally, inflation is calculated year by year on the entire Project Budget, since it can take five to 10 years for some projects to come to fruition. For the purposes of this example, I have assumed inflation for only one year, and only on the Construction Budget. To further simplify matters, I have not included inflation in the Owner's Budget, where it would be calculated separately and included as a line item.

Construction Budget	1 Building Costs	104,615 GSF @ $250/GSF	$26,153,750.00
	2 Fixed Equipment	(8% of Line 1)	$2,092,300.00
	3 Site Development	(15% of Line 1)	$3,923,062.50
	4 Sub Total Construction Budget	(Lines 1+2+3)	$32,169,112.50
	5 Inflation	(4% of Line 4))	$1,286,764.50
	6 Construction Contingency	(5% of Line 4)	$1,608,455.63
	7 Total Construction Budget	(Lines 4+5+6)	$35,064,332.63
Owner's Budget	8 Site Acquisition / Demolition	(Varies - use a plug number)	$500,000.00
	9 FF&E (Movable Equipment)	(Varies - use 10% of Line 4)	$3,216,911.25
	10 Professional Fees	(Varies - use 8% of Line 4)	$2,573,529.00
	11 Design Contingency	(10% of Line 10)	$257,352.90
	12 Administration Costs	(1% of Line 4)	$321,691.13
	13 Subtotal of Owner's Budget	(Lines 8 through 12)	$6,869,484.28
	14 Subtotal of Project Budget	(Lines 7 + 13)	$41,933,816.90
	15 Project Contingency	(5% of Line 14)	$2,096,690.85
Project Budget	16 Total Project Budget Required	(Lines 14 + 15)	$44,030,507.75

Figure 4. Sample Project Budget: Proposed College of Education Building, State University.

Line 6 – Construction Contingency. Since this proposed project is all new construction, the contingency is calculated at 5 percent of the Construction Budget.

Line 7 – Total Construction Budget. The Total Construction Budget is the sum of the Construction Budget plus inflation on the Construction Budget plus the Construction Contingency.

Line 8 – Site Acquisition / Demolition. I have used a plug number for this example. The exact amount would be developed over the course of Pre-Design, and could include the cost of mitigating any hazardous materials present on the proposed site. Such a cost must be included in the Owner's Budget.

Line 9 – Furnishings, Fixtures, and Equipment. As noted earlier, there is little in a project budget that will vary as much with building type as the line item for furnishings, fixtures, and equipment. Even though the rule of thumb for FF&E is 5 percent to 10 percent of the Construction Budget, I selected 10 percent here. In a classroom facility such as our example, classroom furniture and audiovisual equipment would make a sizable demand on the FF&E budget. It's better to be conservative at this stage than to understate the need and be surprised later.

Line 10 – Professional Fees. I have calculated the architectural and engineering (A/E) fees as 8 percent of the Construction Budget, not including inflation and contingency. This is generous for a project of this size, but at this stage I want to make sure that what's available is sufficient.

Line 11 – Design Contingency. The Design Contingency is 10 percent of the A/E fee. On a project involving a new building, it's possible to go with a smaller contingency, say 5 percent. But if, coming out of the Pre-Design stage, there are still many questions about the project scope, a design contingency of 10 percent is wise. The Design Contingency can be reevaluated after the design is completed and the project moves into the Construction

Documents stage. It is the first contingency to be folded back into the Owner's Budget, usually into FF&E.

Line 12 – Administrative Costs. This line item will vary from institution to institution. Some colleges and universities have an administrative "tax" on all projects for institutional physical plant support. At others, the administrative costs are at the state level. If the institution doesn't have its own project management staff, the state agency tasked with public works projects often assesses an administrative "fee" that must be borne by the project. In some cases, the project must bear both costs. Still other institutions charge each capital project a neighborhood or district fee—usually 1–2 percent of the Construction Budget—for "civic" projects, primarily landscaping, site utilities, and infrastructure upgrades in the area of the project.

Line 13 – Subtotal of Owner's Budget. This line item reflects all of the owner's costs.

Line 14 – Subtotal of Project Budget. This line item is arrived at by adding all owner's costs to the Total Construction Budget.

Line 15 – Project Contingency. This contingency is on the entire project, not just construction or design. It covers all unknowns in the process of project development. By the end of the Construction Documents stage and after the project has been bid, decisions can be made about how much, if any, of the Project Contingency can be released to the project. It's always wise to save some of the Project Contingency, but a portion is often applied to bid alternates.

Line 16 – Total Project Budget Required. This is the amount required to accomplish all aspects of the proposed facility project. This sample budget reflects a slightly smaller than normal ratio of Owner's Budget to Construction Budget, around 21 percent Owner's vs. 79 percent Construction.

Project Schedule

The last Pre-Design element to be discussed is the Project Schedule. Though we are discussing it last, it should be developed concurrently with the rest of the Pre-design effort. At this point, the project schedule is little more than a best-case scenario for how long each stage of the process will take. There are still agreements to be made, budgets to be approved, and funding to be secured, all of which will take more time than you anticipate. A typical milestone bullet schedule would look something like the one shown in Figure 5.

A more "graphic" type of schedule would show time spans in relation to each other. This kind of schedule is easier for most people to read and helps them visualize the time frames involved. (See Figure 6)

Pre-Design Conclusion

The steps in the Pre-Design process that we have discussed include:

- Establishing a planning committee.
- Defining the problem and identifying project origination.
- Defining the exact need that is to be met by this project.
- Establishing the parameters of that need.
- Coordinating the project with institutional policy.
- Creating a project program.

Milestone:	Date:
A/E Team Selected & Assembled	September 13, 1996
A/E Negotiations & Contract finalized	October 1, 1996
Program Scope & Verification	Oct. 7 to Jan. 15, 1997
Schematic Design	Mar. 7 to May 2, 1997
Design Development	May 2 to Aug 8, 1997
Construction Documents on Commons	Aug. 15 to Jan 15, 1 1998
Institutional & State Reviews	Feb 1998
Bidding	March 1998
Negotiations	April 1998
Construction of Commons	May 1998 to January 2000
Beneficial Occupancy of Commons	January 2000

Figure 5. Schedule

- Creating a project budget.
- Creating a project schedule.

A successful Pre-Design process sets the stage for all that follows. The more comprehensive and thorough the Pre-Design, the easier the next stage—Design will be.

One final comment on the Pre-Design stage. Sometimes administrators and others involved in the capital project process have what I call a "project-centric" view of the world. The only thing that matters is getting the project designed and built, and any activity perceived as detracting from that focus is thrust aside in the headlong rush toward completion. But you, your institution, and those who follow you will have to live with the results of your capital project process for the next 50 to 100 years. The Pre-Design stage of a proj-

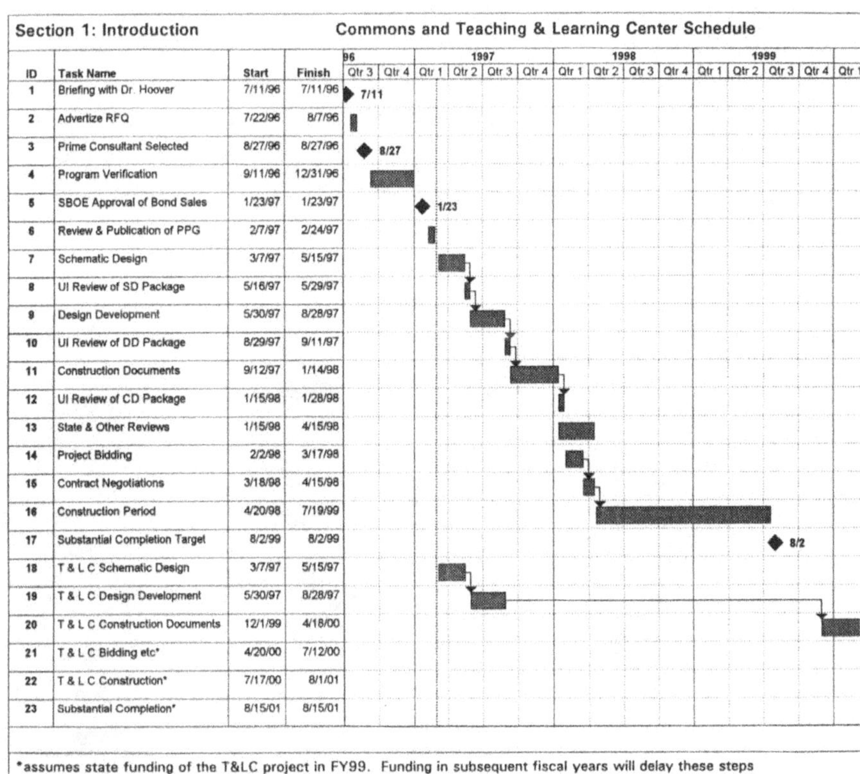

Section 1: Introduction — Commons and Teaching & Learning Center Schedule

ID	Task Name	Start	Finish
1	Briefing with Dr. Hoover	7/11/96	7/11/96
2	Advertize RFQ	7/22/96	8/7/96
3	Prime Consultant Selected	8/27/96	8/27/96
4	Program Verification	9/11/96	12/31/96
5	SBOE Approval of Bond Sales	1/23/97	1/23/97
6	Review & Publication of PPG	2/7/97	2/24/97
7	Schematic Design	3/7/97	5/15/97
8	UI Review of SD Package	5/16/97	5/29/97
9	Design Development	5/30/97	8/28/97
10	UI Review of DD Package	8/29/97	9/11/97
11	Construction Documents	9/12/97	1/14/98
12	UI Review of CD Package	1/15/98	1/28/98
13	State & Other Reviews	1/15/98	4/15/98
14	Project Bidding	2/2/98	3/17/98
15	Contract Negotiations	3/18/98	4/15/98
16	Construction Period	4/20/98	7/19/99
17	Substantial Completion Target	8/2/99	8/2/99
18	T & L C Schematic Design	3/7/97	5/15/97
19	T & L C Design Development	5/30/97	8/28/97
20	T & L C Construction Documents	12/1/99	4/18/00
21	T & L C Bidding etc*	4/20/00	7/12/00
22	T & L C Construction*	7/17/00	8/1/01
23	Substantial Completion*	8/15/01	8/15/01

*assumes state funding of the T&LC project in FY99. Funding in subsequent fiscal years will delay these steps

Figure 6. Graphically Displayed Schedule

ect is critical not only to the short-term process of designing and building a facility, but also to the long-term process of its occupancy and functional life. It bears repeating that errors, omissions, and oversights in the Pre-Design / planning phase tend to become embedded in the design, and the consequences ripple across the life of a project, often plaguing the facility's users for years. Making sure you spend sufficient resources—including time—in the Pre-Design stage will produce dividends down the road. An extra 30 or 45 days spent programming and defining the project is less than one-tenth of 1 percent of the overall life of the facility, but it will make a huge difference in its success. Research by the Independent Project Analysis Corporation has shown that a poorly defined project costs 17 percent more than the average, while a well defined project costs 20 percent less.[15] These figures alone should prompt better Pre-Design efforts.

Again, the Pre-Design stage is when the non-architect has the greatest opportunity for a positive impact on the outcome of the project. (See Figure 7) As it progresses through the next stages of Schematic Design and Design Development, the project moves into the hands of the design consultant and you will have fewer chances for input.

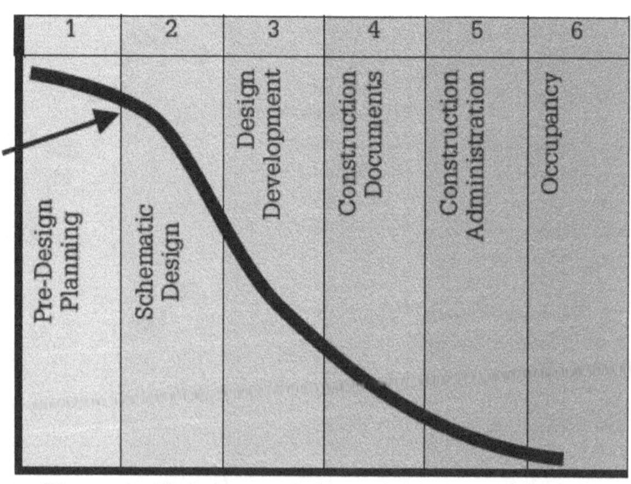

Figure 7. Ability to Influence Project Outcomes

Chapter 2
The Design Process

The Design Process includes three phases: **Schematic Design**, **Design Development,** and **Construction Documents**. If the Pre-Design phase was completed "in-house" by institutional staff, it will be necessary to engage an architectural consultant to complete the subsequent phases. If the Pre-Design phase was accomplished through a consultancy, the project could be completed with the same consultant, provided the consultant is qualified and that institutional policy and/or state regulations permit the hiring of the same consultant to complete both the Pre-Design and the Design phases. If the Pre-Design consultant isn't qualified, doesn't have the staffing, or isn't legally allowed to continue with the project, another consultant must be secured. The following information outlines how to select a consultant.

The first step in securing design services is usually issuing a "Request for Proposal" or "RFP." The other option is to issue an "RFQ" or "Request for Qualifications." Though they are technically different, most institutions and design firms treat them the same. The consultant's response to an RFP or RFQ is called an "SOQ," i.e. "Statement of Qualifications," or simply the "Proposal." Most states regulate what must be included in RFPs published by state agencies and institutions. Private institutions don't have the same requirements, but the following information is useful for both. A good RFP will include the following elements:

- Institutional and Project Background

- Project Scope Description
- Minimum Qualifications of Consultants
- Fee Basis
- Project Schedule
- Proposal Evaluation

Background

Include background information on the institution and a brief background of the project in your RFP. This can be as little as a paragraph. The background of the institution is usually boilerplate, provided by the institution and the same in every RFP. The background of the project should include the building type (classroom building, dormitory, laboratory, or office building) and where the money is coming from (state funds, federal funds, private donations, bond-generated revenue, or a combination of the above.). Remember, where a project's funding originates often defines, or at least influences, how it is delivered. If it is known, what you think the project budget amount may be should also be included.

Scope Description

This is a description of what type or kind of facility it is, and its size and "flavor," if you know it. This can include information like the targeted gross square feet, style of architecture, building type, and any applicable institutional design guidelines and standards.

Minimum Qualifications

What are the minimum qualifications that you want the consultants to have? Do you want them to have had project experience with this specific building type? Do you want them to have done at least five projects of this kind? Do you want the team to include not just engineers but also landscape architects, interior designers, and an audio-visual consultant? Shall the consultant team be led by an architect? Or shall a landscape architect or urban planner lead the team? If it's a laboratory facility, will a lab planning specialist lead the team? Will the successful candidate be a local or in-state architect, or can an out-of-state architect submit an SOQ?

Fee Basis

Is the institution going to propose paying a percentage of construction or a stipulated fee? Let them know up front how you plan to do business. As mentioned in Chapter 1, consultant selection should never be based on a proposed or potential fee, but rather on the basis of the consultant's qualifications. Fees are dynamic and can be negotiated; qualifications are fairly constant. I have spoken with many architects about this and they all agree. Leslie Loudon, project manager for Little Diversified Architectural Consulting, headquartered in Charlotte, North Carolina, said it best: "Selecting firms on qualifications will yield better results than asking for fee proposals in the selection process. Clients will get better value by focusing on qualifications. Firms selected for their low fees often have to take a less 'hands-on' approach to serving their clients and are much more likely to need to charge additional service fees for small changes during

What do architects like to see in an RFQs scope description?

"A general scope of work, usually mentioning the approximate budget and high-level descriptor of the project but not much else. Many RFQs don't provide enough information for the consultant to focus on client needs but require a broad listing of skills that may never be used when developing a project (if selected)."

—Ted Weidner, President,
Facility Asset Consulting

"Description of the project scope and budget and the client's over-arching goals/vision for the facility."

—Leslie Louden, Project Manager,
Little Diversified Architectural Consulting

"A vision statement about the project by the institution that is backed up and supported by the decision makers. A clear short list of the client's greatest concerns and if possible size and budget of the project."

—Alan Cuteri, Architect,
Strada Architecture LLC

the design process. This can bog down the design schedule and cost the client more money in the end."

Suggestions from a Consultant on Proposal Evaluation:

"Don't make the whole thing more work than it needs to be, i.e. requiring more paperwork than can be effectively evaluated by a building committee and multiple interviews. Don't ask for more than you can use just because it is typically done. Nobody can read 25 phone book-size proposals."

—Christie Coffin,
Senior Architect
The Design Partnership

Suggestions from a Client on Proposal Evaluation:

"Look closely at the projects they have completed. Do the buildings have a common trait that does NOT fit your campus? Nothing is worse than having an architect build THEIR building and put you in it rather than really designing a building that fits the program and prevailing character of campus."

—Lynette Jones
Senior Facilities Planner
West Virginia University

Schedule

What is the timeline, not just for when the proposal is due, but for the evaluation of the proposals, the interviews, the design process, and construction of the project? Are there are "drop-dead" dates that the consultant should know about up front? For instance, if the project is financed by bond revenues, what is the date by which all funds must be expended before arbitrage begins? If the funds are from a grant, is there a date at which all funds have to be committed or expended? Does the construction have to be completed before the start of a particular academic term?

Proposal Evaluation

It is only fair to the consultants submitting on the project (and in some states it's required by law) to let them know how you are planning to evaluate their proposals. In many cases, proposal evaluation looks to consultants like "black-box decision-making": the proposal disappears into the institutional black box and what goes on in there is hidden until someone emerges with a decision.

One simple way to make the evaluation process faster and easier is to limit the number of pages in the consultant proposal. This forces the consultants to really think through what should be in their proposals. You should also let the consultant know what counts against the page limit and what doesn't. I agree with Judith Sayler's suggestion (See Box) that résumés not be counted against the limit, but included in an appendix to the proposal. I would also suggest that reference letters be included in the proposal but not counted against the page limit.

> *"If there are page limits set, be clear as to what is counted in the page limit and what is not. Because résumés of key personnel are probably the most important thing in a proposal and are what interests clients the most, the more detailed they are, the better. But if they are counted as part of the page limits they will often be short and leave out important information. It is better to have résumés in an appendix and not part of the page count."*
>
> —Judith Sayler, VP
> Business Development,
> Don Todd Associates Inc.

Other Considerations

There are a variety of ways to solicit proposals:

- You can advertise in local newspapers, trade journals and periodicals.
- You can send general announcements to your state or regional American Institute of Architects (AIA) membership.
- You can send targeted solicitations to just a few firms. Most public institutions would be unable to do this unless the firms had been pre-qualified. One difficulty in sending targeted solicitations is deciding how many firms to solicit. You want to send enough to generate responses, but not so many as to overwhelm the process.

SELECTING A CONSULTANT

Selecting a Consultant

"Facile remedium est ubertati; sterilia nullo labore vincuntur."

—Quintilian

("Exuberance is easily corrected; dullness is incurable.")

What to Look For in a Consultant

One of your most important decisions will be what kind of firm you want to design your project. Do you want a "starchitect" (an architectural "star")? Do you want a smaller local firm or a large national one? There are distinct advantages and disadvantages to each of these options. Large firms have the wider technical and support resources. Although they may have fewer resources, small firms and sole proprietors tend to be "hungrier" and generally provide more of themselves and their talents to the client. Lynette Jones, a senior facilities planner at West Virginia University, suggests that what matters isn't so much the size of the firm as its location. She says it "works best if the architect is located within a two-hour drive of campus." This proximity enhances communication. Although you'll pay more for a large firm coming from far away, that doesn't necessarily guarantee that the local firm is a "deal," either. My personal preference is for small, hungry firms with design talent. I would rather ratchet back a talented designer than try to goad a mediocre one to excellence. To quote the Roman orator Quintilian, "Exuberance is easily corrected; dullness is incurable." What's more, I would rather pay for and get a small firm's first string than pay a large firm's first-string prices and get their second-string talent, or sometimes even their third string.

If your project is, for instance, a student recreation center, you would obviously look for a firm that has experience with recreation centers, but maybe not a firm that's done 25 of them. If you select a firm that's never done your building type, you will pay for their learning curve. But if they've done 25 buildings similar to yours, you risk getting an architect who's bored with the building type and delivers a "rubber stamp" project. In my opinion, the ideal firm is one that is well along the learning curve, but not over it yet.

The Consultant's Viewpoint

Consider these points:

- When they call you or visit you, they are always looking for work, always "on," always marketing. Don't be offended by that. They're trying to put food on the table, just like you.
- They're looking for as much information as they can get to prepare their proposal and/or for an interview. If you give information to one potential proposer, you must give it to all proposers. The Golden Rule applies in this situation: be fair to all. The best policy is to not give out any information beyond that already specified in the RFP. However, talented architects ask better questions and will look for information that was, perhaps inadvertently, left out of the RFP. The fairest solution is to have what is called a "pre-proposal conference," to which all potential proposers are invited. At that time, the institution or agency can make a thorough presentation about the project and answer all questions. Everyone in attendance gets to hear the same information. Just make sure that the pre-proposal conference is held at least three weeks in advance of the RFP due date so that information learned in the conference can be reflected in the SOQ. An alternative to the pre-proposal conference, or in conjunction with it, is suggested by Judith Sayler, vice president for business development at Don Todd Associates: "If you have a website, make the RFP and addenda available as a PDF on the website. You can also post questions and answers on the website as well. If there are master plans or other reports about the project, post those as well." This option gives all consultants the same access to pertinent information, even if they can't attend the pre-proposal conference.
- Architects and designers will pursue every project they have a reasonable chance to get, but it isn't cheap to prepare proposals. Don't ask for material that you're not going to read or review. All too often, consultants prepare propos-

als that cost thousands of dollars but go unread and unreviewed, because the selection process had a foregone conclusion.

Suggestions from a Consultant on Shortlisting Firms:

"Develop a true 'shortlist' of firms (three to four maximum, not six or seven) to be selected for interviews."

—Leslie Loudon,
Project Manager,
Little Diversified
Architecture

Suggestions from a Client on Shortlisting Firms:

"Don't interview more than four firms. We interviewed six for a $52 million dollar project and it was completely mind-numbing. You can't continue to be objective."

—Lynette Jones,
Senior Facility Planner,
West Virginia University

Shortlisting Firms

After reviewing and evaluating proposals, it is customary to create a "shortlist" of firms to interview for the work. You should be convinced that any firm on the shortlist would be able to accomplish your project. How many firms should be shortlisted? Most consultants will tell you the fewer the better; every consultant I surveyed suggested a shortlist of no more than four firms. I've seen shortlists that had as many as eight firms. My preference is for a shortlist of three to five: the smaller the project, the shorter the shortlist. The interview process isn't cheap for either the consultant or the institutional members of the selection committee. Many firms will invest tens of thousands of dollars to prepare for an interview. If they really don't have a chance, don't shortlist them.

Another step that should be accomplished prior to completing a shortlist is the checking of references. Doing this after the interviews is a mistake. Checking references can help you create the shortlist. Alec Holser, a partner in Opsis Architecture, Portland, Oregon, notes that this important step is too often neglected altogether.

Interviews

All firms that submitted proposals should be notified of who made the shortlist. The firms on the shortlist should be notified of the time and place for interviews. Give them a minimum of three weeks' lead-time so they can make travel arrangements, if necessary, and prepare materials, which may include reports, drawings, models, and/or computer presentations.

> *"What usually makes or breaks a project is the client/consultant chemistry."*
>
> —John Ullberg
> Landscape Architect
> Cornell University

Several considerations should be taken into account in establishing the time and place for the interview:

- Every member of the selection committee should be in attendance at every interview. It isn't fair to the consultants and it skews the results if any selection committee members are absent. Any committee member who can't make it to every interview should excuse himself or herself from the process.
- If possible, hold all interviews in the same room. This levels the playing field and eliminates the risk that the environment might unduly influence the selection committee or give one team an unfair advantage.
- If possible, hold all interviews on the same day, or at least within a two-day period. This allows the selection committee to compare presentations that are fresh in their minds.
- Establishing interview order is a thankless job. Most firms want to go either first or last. No one wants to be buried in the middle. One reasonable way to establish interview order is to allow the firm that is traveling the farthest to choose the time that will work best with its travel needs. A truly fair method for scheduling the order is with a random drawing of firm names from a coffee cup. Just remember that however the interview order is established, someone will be displeased.
- Make sure that the interview room is large enough for the firms to set up display boards, and that all selection commit-

tee members have clear sight lines to the presentations. Most firms will appreciate the opportunity to see the room prior to the interview in order to better plan their presentation.

During the interview, "focus on work style rather than qualifications, which were clearly stated in the written submission. If we're shortlisted for an interview, then we ought to be qualified and the focus should be on 'chemistry' between the client and us."

—Ted Weidner, President,
Facility Asset Consulting

"Interviews should be long enough for the committee to get a sense of expertise of the team and to determine if there is a good chemistry between the team and the committee:

- *Introductions of the committee and by the team: 5 minutes:*
- *Consultant team presentation: 30–40 minutes:*
- *Questions and answers or enough time for each committee member to ask at least one question: 30–45 minutes, for a total of 65 to 90 minutes"*

—Bob Sena
Senior Planner
Moore, Iacofano, Goltsman

- Some firms will make their entire presentation with audiovisual equipment—laptop computers and projectors, or even slide projectors. This means the room should have, or have access to, a screen or other audiovisual equipment. If the room has windows, they should have the capability of being darkened.
- Most firms will appreciate the opportunity to rearrange the room for their presentation. If you allow one firm that opportunity, allow all firms to do it. Simply provide sufficient time between interviews for the room to be set up and tell the consultants how much time they will have. John White, director of capital planning at the University of California, Merced, suggests keeping the consultants separated so they don't run into each other, thus avoiding potential awkwardness.

- Provide refreshments for the selection committee and the interviewees. Sometimes firms bring refreshments with them in an effort to influence the process. If the institution or agency conducting the interviews provides the refreshments, it obviates any advantage sought by the firms.
- Handle campus logistics for the consultant teams. Even for a consultant team familiar with your campus, Bob Sena of Moore Iacofano Goltsman, Berkeley, CA, says providing a map of campus, directions for parking and finding the interview room, and a visitor's parking pass well in advance of the visit is extremely helpful. (Think about it: you would do the same for a person you were interviewing for a staff position in your department. In this case, you're interviewing someone for a "temporary" position with your institution—so be nice to them.)

I'm a firm believer in interviews, and the longer the better; I like two-hour interviews. (Long interviews are another justification for smaller shortlists.) The reason for long interviews is that you're going to be working with these consultants for at least three to four years, and much longer with some projects. The interview is your chance to see what kind of chemistry your team will have with their team. Let the consultants have plenty of time to make their presentation, and reserve plenty of time for questions and answers. Watch group dynamics before and after the interview. Do their team members relate well with each other? Does the consultant team interact well with your team? One informal way to measure interaction chemistry is what I call the "humor index." I have participated in dozens of interviews and often would count the number of times a firm would make jokes during the presentation. Sometimes the jokes were at their expense, sometimes at the institution's expense. I found that the firm that made us laugh the most won the job 98 percent of the time. While not a scientific or unbiased study, it does illustrate that humor is a measure of the firm's communication skills, relational skills and general amiability.

Consider options other than a traditional interview, such as conducting the interview in the consultant's office, touring some of their completed facilities, and interviewing their previous clients. Bruce Blackmer, CEO of Northwest Architectural Company, with offices in Spokane and Seattle, Washington, offers this wisdom on the subject of interviews:

> Once firm credentials and capabilities have been reviewed and a shortlist of qualified firms established, the 'people fit' becomes the most important consideration. A short interview is the typical mode of making a selection, but it is very difficult to truly evaluate the likelihood of a long, successful relationship in the 30- to 60-minute interview held by most institutions. A successful method has been to visit the architects' office and tour one or more of their relevant projects with the architect and preferably the owner present. You are establishing a partnership . . . don't shortchange yourself of a thorough evaluation. Allow adequate time for questions, answers, and discussion during the interview. Remember you are evaluating the potentials of a relationship, so tailor the interview to seek out how that relationship will work, not just to have a 'dog & pony' show.
>
> Recognize that an interview is an 'artificial situation' created in an attempt to predict future performance. The skill set primarily needed for future project success has little in common with the 'theater arts' that have become so typical in many interviews. Don't be afraid to limit the formal aspects of the interview in particular and look for ways in which you can really get to know the team.

Post-Interview Debriefing

Once the selection committee has completed its deliberations and a winning team has been selected, it is usually appropriate to notify institutional leadership of the decision before notifying the teams. All teams, not just the winners, should be notified of the outcome. While it's always fun to call the winning team, notifying the losers can be awkward. Sometimes it's done with a call, often with a letter. Some institutions never notify the losing teams; the absence of the "winning" call is the *de facto* notification. I find that rude and unprofessional. If you thought enough of the team's qualifications to shortlist them and interview them, they likewise deserve the consideration of a phone call notifying them of the outcome of the interviews.

The firms that aren't successful in the interview process often will seek a debriefing to ascertain why they weren't selected. Losing a job is a painful experience, but seeking to learn from the failure is an admirable and necessary aspect of both personal and professional growth. Sometimes state or institutional regulations prohibit post-interview debriefings, but if it is allowed and you do choose to do it, there are several points to keep in mind:

- Be aware of potential legal pitfalls. Even if the debriefing process is allowed, make sure your legal counsel is aware that you're going to do it and find out what guidelines they have for you.
- Be as honest as you can. Sugar-coating issues won't help the team on their next interview.
- Be aware that even though it can be painful for everyone involved, most consultants would rather go through a negative debriefing than continue to lose jobs.

"Recognize that architects are professionals who spend a lot of time doing these proposals. Communicate with them in a timely and professional way—even if it is to say, 'Sorry, we're giving the job to someone else.'"

Fran Gast, AVP Facilities Planning, Rhode Island School of Design

Negotiating Contracts

In addition to the call that notifies the winning team, an official letter of notification is sent as well, outlining next steps. The first "next step" is to define the scope of work and negotiate the contract. This will take longer than you think. Don't scrimp on consultant compensation—you get what you pay for. As mentioned previously, some states prescribe the amount of compensation allowed. Remember, too, that the AIA's contract formulas define "basic services" as well as "special" or "additional" services. Be sure that all the services you need, basic or special, are included in the contract. For instance, creating artist's renderings or models of the proposed facility for use in marketing and fundraising is not a basic service. If you determine that these are needed, include them in the contract negotiation as a special service. Always engage qualified institutional legal representation when negotiating and signing any contract.

"Clara pacta, boni amici."

("Clear agreements, good friends.")

SCHEMATIC DESIGN

Once your consultants are hired and on board, their first step will be to review all the documentation from your in-house Pre-Design process to make sure that they fully understand what you're seeking and the scope and assumptions of the project. Don't be offended by this—it's their way of performing "due diligence."

Consultants use a variety of methods to ferret out what they think are the design determinants of a project, those elements that will shape it and give it form. One method is to have extensive meetings with the project planning committee. Another is to hold a variety of meetings or workshops, sometimes called "squatter sessions" or focus groups, in order to gather information informally from user groups and other stakeholders. (The term "squatter" comes from the notion of everyone involved in the project squatting in a circle and talking about it.) These sessions are designed to ensure the consultants that they've gathered all pertinent data, and that all parties affected by the project have the opportunity to voice their opinions and concerns.

Input, Review, and Decision Authority

It is vital to articulate the distinctions between *input* authority, *review* authority, and *decision* authority early in the life of a project, so that everyone knows where they stand. Any stakeholder affected by the project—including off-campus community constituents—should have *input* authority. These opinions usually come in squatter sessions or public design review sessions. But having input doesn't imply the right to *review* the project at every stage or to expect that all their opinions will be heeded. Only the views of those who will be directly impacted by the project, immediate neighbors and occupants, need be considered by the design team. Beyond that, there must be an ultimate authority that renders *decisions* and provides direction to the consultant team. Part of the institutional representative's role is to help the consultants distinguish between the opinions that should carry weight in the process and those that shouldn't. Issues of critical importance to the institution and to the project take precedence over issues of importance to an individual or even a particular stakeholder group. Ultimately, someone at the institution has to make those calls and provide direction to the consultant team—that's *decision* authority.

Products of Schematic Design

After the first series of workshops or squatter sessions, the architects will proceed with Schematic Design (SD). The first products of Schematic Design will of course vary with the designer and process followed, but they are likely to include schematic diagrams such as adjacency and relational matrixes, circulation and flow diagrams (usually pedestrian and vehicular), and bubble diagrams. These diagrams don't describe what the building will look like. Rather, they illustrate how the architect proposes to arrange elements of the building to solve functional and relational problems between various aspects of the architectural program.

Adjacency Matrix

An adjacency matrix is a way to array in a tabular form both the relationships between functions and the functions' relationships to other criteria, such as hours of operation, access to sunlight, etc. (See Figure 8)

Circulation Diagrams

Circulation diagrams begin to array how people, equipment, and vehicles may move about the site and in and through the pro-

PROGRAM AREA	Adjacencies to Pedestrian Traffic H=High Traffic M=Moderate Traffic L=Little Traffic	Adjacency to Programmed Outdoor Space D=Direct N=Nearby R=Removed	Hours of Use 24 hours/day 16 hours/day 8-10 hours /day	Building Security S=Most Secure M=Medium N=Normal	Service Access F=Frequent & Bulky M=Moderate L=Light
Student Services					
Vice President Student Affairs	M	R	10	M	L
Dean of Student Services	M	R	10	M	L
Student Disability Services	M	R	10	M	L
Women's Center	M	R	10	M	L
Multi-Cultural Center	M	R	10	M	L
Math and Statistics Advising Center	M	R	16	M	L
Tutoring and Acad. Assist. Center	M	R	16	M	L
Student Support Services	M	R	16	M	L
Coop Education	M	R	10	M	L
Honors Program	M	R	16	M	L
Writing Center	M	R	16	M	L
Student Activities					
Associated Students of UI	M				
Student Organizations					
Student Media					

Figure 8. Example of an Adjacency Matrix

posed facility. They highlight the physical constraints and opportunities in designing circulation for the project. (See Figure 9)

Bubble Diagrams
Bubble diagrams are graphic representations of adjacency matrices. Each bubble is sized according to how much square footage the function it represents may require. These diagrams show the relationships between functions and how they might be arranged in actual physical locations. (See Figure 10)

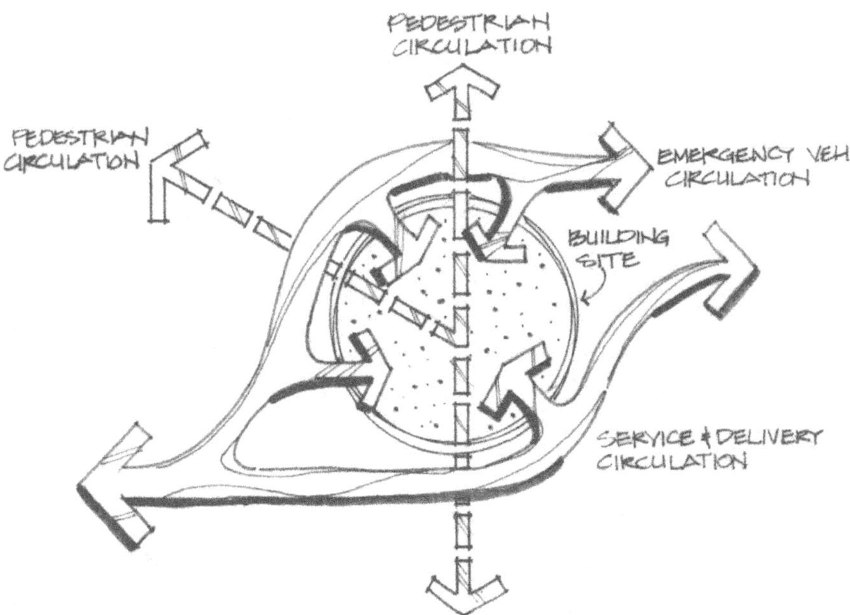

Figure 9. Circulation Diagram

Once the designer has begun to explore and resolve some of the problems in a diagrammatic way, he or she will proceed to the next phase of the Schematic Design stage, which includes concept diagrams, building diagrams, and massing models.

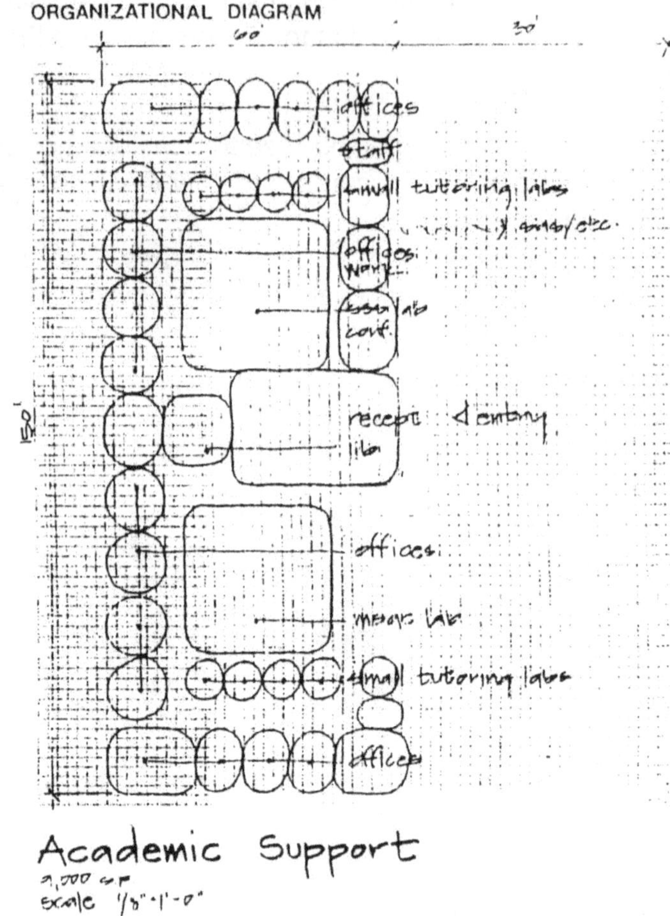

Figure 10. Bubble Diagram developed from Adjacency Matrix

Concept Diagrams

Concept diagrams take bubble diagrams to the next level. They show more of what an actual floor plan might look like. Sometimes a concept diagram will also take an abstract concept or symbolic analogy and link it to a building image or form. (See Figure 11)

Building Diagrams

Building diagrams begin to show actual floor plan details, giving form in an approximate way to ideas that were previously expressed conceptually in bubble diagrams. Though usually drawn to scale, their purpose is more to explore functional adjacencies and design possibilities than to indicate hard and fast design decisions. While it may seem odd that the drawings and plans are so "loose" or sketchy, that is intentional. At this stage of the project, it's still important to keep ideas and forms a little

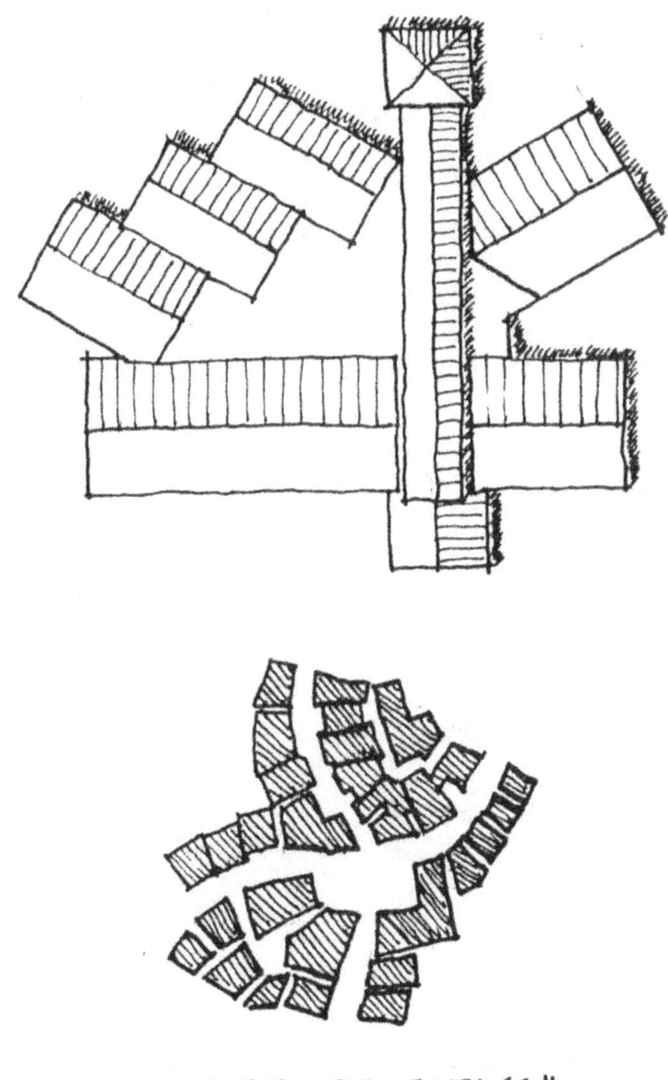

Figure 11. Concept Diagram

unfinished and unresolved to allow for flexibility. If the design moves too quickly to a hard-lined drawing, further ideation and exploration can be short-circuited. (See Figure 12)

Massing Models / Study Models

Using clay, wood, or foam-core boards, architects may begin to develop what are called massing models. These begin to tell you, without a lot of detail, what form the building will take: its general mass (hence the name), the volume of enclosed spaces, roof forms, and relationships to exterior spaces and surrounding buildings.

Reviewing Schematic Designs

In my mind, Schematic Design is the really fun stage of the process because the architects have been busy doing what they do best: being creative. The first time you get to see what the architects have been working on is a thrilling moment. Honestly,

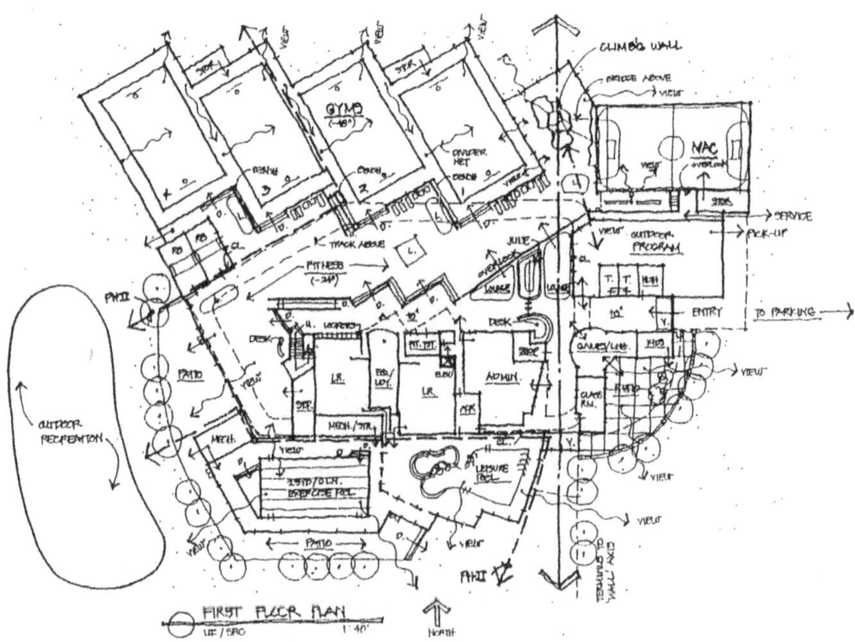

Figure 12. Building Diagram

it feels a little like a blind date! You're excited to see what they have, but at the same time a little apprehensive. It's especially exciting if you've asked them to think outside the box and come

What is the highlight of working with architects?

"Those moments when the architect takes a mutually explored idea to a higher plane."

—John Ullberg
Landscape Architect
Cornell University

"Good architects can translate a program—a set of needs—into something that really works as beautiful three-dimensional space. Too often clients want to present solutions instead of define their problems. Let the architects do what they do well—solve problems. The good ones will come up with solutions you never imagined."

—Fran Gast
Assistant Vice President, Facilities Planning
Rhode Island School of Design

"Certainly the creative process is the highlight. When architects are able to translate words and vision statements into building concepts that make sense, then you feel like you are really getting somewhere."

—Zelinda Zingaro
Senior Project Manager
San Francisco State University

"The excitement of working with really creative people who are proud of what they do and the legacy they will leave behind. The translation of sometimes vague ideas into physical form can seem magical."

—Celia Kent
Director, Faculty of Arts and Sciences Office
Harvard University

up with creative solutions to your design problem—they are really good at "outside the box." And if that's what you asked for, don't be offended when they come back with a solution that is, indeed, "outside the box."

It's easy to base initial reactions on the appearance of the building, and that's usually a mistake. Curtis Moody, president and CEO of Moody Nolan Inc., Columbus, Ohio, suggests that you "first review the functional adjacencies, making sure that the operational needs have been addressed. Do this before reviewing exterior concepts." Edward Tuttle, in his book, *With Benefit of Architect*, also cautions against hasty reactions. He likens reviewing a design to becoming more familiar with a new acquaintance. A good-looking person may appear less so once you get to know them and find that you really don't like them. By the same token, a homely person may become more attractive as you discover their fine personal qualities. So look for how the spaces function: Are all the programmatic needs met? Are circulation patterns clear? Are all important adjacencies addressed in the layout of the spaces? Satisfy yourself that the plan works before reviewing the exterior appearance of the facility.

Final SD Review and Budget Reconciliation

After they're reviewed and accepted by the client, the architect will choose the one or two favored concepts developed through schematic design and cost them out at the level of detail available. This will lead to a final presentation wherein all the elements of Schematic Design are presented and the budget reconciled. It is not uncommon at this stage for the proposed cost of the facility to be between 5 percent and 20 percent out of balance with the proposed budget. Don't panic—there are too many unknowns at this point for a design team to pin down an exact cost. However, if the estimate is more than 25 percent over the budget, you may need to re-scope the project before moving forward. At this stage, cost estimates are based on unit prices rather than the square-foot costs used in the Pre-Design effort.

Another valuable option to pursue at this stage is a third-party cost estimate. There are consultants who are experts in cost estimating; it's all they do.

Depending on the complexity of the project and the quality of the Pre-Design effort, the Schematic Design phase should last 90 to 120 days. The final product of this phase should be a written report including all necessary graphic materials to support it. Sometimes this stage will also produce perspective drawings (or an 'artist's rendering' of the project) and/or models that can be used in publications and fund-raising efforts.

DESIGN DEVELOPMENT

At the end of the Schematic Design phase, and upon receipt, review, and acceptance of the SD Report, the consultant is usually authorized to move one concept into the Design Development phase, a.k.a. "DD." Occasionally, two or more concepts will be carried forward to be further developed, but that exploration should be resolved quickly in order to focus on one option.

Refining the Plan and the Budget

The purpose of the Design Development phase is to develop, refine, and complete the design concept developed in Schematic Design. Schematic Design was focused on the physical relationship of functions and developed those relationships primarily in plan view. DD begins to integrate all the disciplines: architecture, landscape architecture, electrical, mechanical, structural, interiors, and specialists. Coordinating these disciplines is critical; this is where project architects really earn their keep.

Many unknowns of the project process are finally resolved during DD. Decisions are made about the quality and level of finishes, materials, and systems in the building, allowing the client to see the project in much more detail. This also results in seeing the budget in much more detail. At this stage, the project will inevitably be 5 percent to 10 percent over budget. That's probably an acceptable level of overage, but if the project is more than 20 percent over budget, it may be time to seriously consider rescoping.

Many architectural firms have in-house cost estimators whose sole job is to develop cost estimates from the drawings. In the absence of a specialist, architects themselves will prepare cost estimates. Regardless of their role in the firm, they may consciously or unconsciously skew their estimates to place the firm or the project in a positive light. To preclude this, many clients hire independent third-party cost consultants at this stage. In fact, some states require third-party cost estimating on projects. This isn't meant as an affront to architects or a slighting of their abilities. It simply recognizes that a fresh set of eyes on a project can be invaluable.

If the estimated construction costs exceed the budget at the end of Design Development, clients sometimes turn to "value engineering," a.k.a. "VE." The following definition of value engineering is from Arizona State University's *Capital Project Management Group Policies and Procedures Manual*[16]:

> An organized approach to optimizing both cost and performance in a facility or to eliminating items that add cost without contributing to required function. In evaluating the quality, use, life, appearance, and required features of a facility, the consultant attempts to achieve value without reducing quality below required levels while at the same time maximizing function, cost, and worth in design.[17]

Value engineering, at least as used at this stage of the process, is essentially a cost reduction methodology rather than a design exercise. Its sole function is to eliminate a $10 widget from the project when a $3.75 widget will suffice. Too often, the lower-cost widget lacks some of the aesthetic features of the $10 widget, which tends to give VE a negative connotation. However, many argue that VE should be an integral part of the design process rather than a cost-reduction strategy added late in Design Development. In either case, it is vital to fully consider the life-cycle cost of materials and "widgets" (whatever they may be). More often than not, initial savings translate into higher maintenance or replacement costs in the future. Long-term and aesthetic value should be the driver in VE, not just the initial bottom line.

Products of the Design Development Stage

Whereas SD graphic products were diagrammatic, sketchy, evocative, and conceptual, (See Figure 12) the graphic products of DD will be much more detailed. (See Figure 13) They will pin down sizes and forms and materials. In addition to fully developed plan views, DD products will include elevations (showing the various faces of the buildings), sections, models, color and material boards, and perspectives. (See Appendix A: Understanding Design Documents) They will also include specifications, the detailed written instructions to a contractor on how to build the project. Specifications are considered formal, legal documents and carry more consequence than the drawings. At this stage, they will be in outline form.

The DD phase can typically run 120 days. Cost estimates should be based on a construction cost breakdown of labor and materials and will have an accuracy level of ± 5–10 percent.

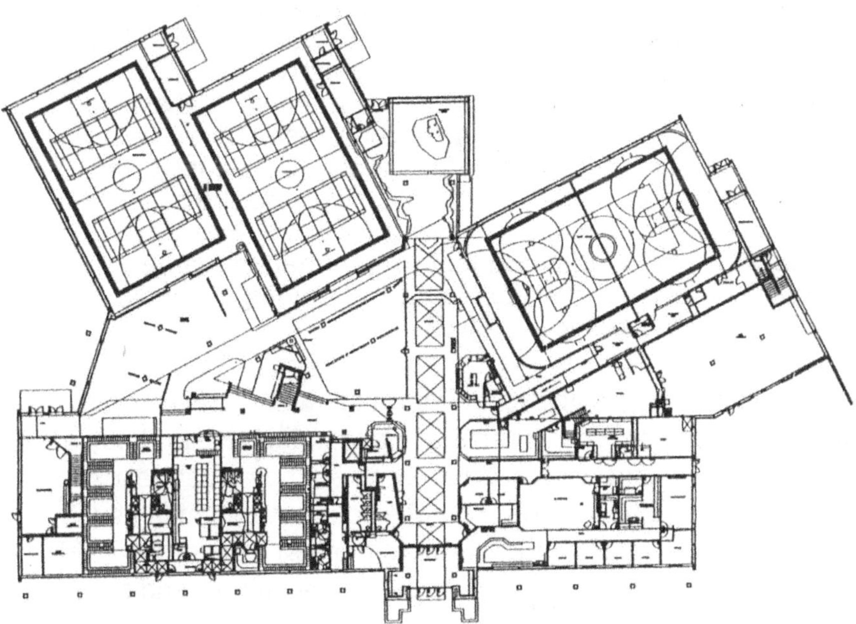

Figure 13. Design Development Drawing

Construction Documents

CONSTRUCTION DOCUMENTS

The final phase in the design stage of a project is the production of Construction Documents (sometimes also called Contract Documents) or "CDs." Construction Documents comprise both drawings and specifications. Other products of the CD phase include bid packages and the final cost estimate and budget reconciliation.

Construction Document drawings are, of course, the graphic representation of how a contractor is to build the new facility. CD specifications are written instructions to the same end. Together, they represent the culmination of the design process. Unlike SD or DD documents, CDs form the basis for the formal, legal contract between the owner and the contractor. In case of a discrepancy or conflict between the drawings and the specifications, the written instructions take precedence. Edward Allen, author of *How Buildings Work*, describes CDs this way:

> The specifications and working drawings are, for all practical purposes, the sole means of translating the design ideas of the owner and architect into an actual building. They serve as the basis on which construction financing is granted, the basis for various insurances, the basis for estimating and bidding construction costs, the basis for the general construction contract and all subcontracts, the basis for material supply contracts, and the basis for a legal permit to build the building. As such they must be complete, clear, unambiguous, and understandable. . . . Beauty is of no importance in these drawings, but clarity and precision are.[18]

Construction drawings are very detailed, incredibly complex documents, and it takes a certain knack to read them. They are what the contractor uses to build from, so they must be accurate, clear, and understandable . . . for the contractor, which usually means that the uninitiated (all the rest of us) have difficulty deciphering them. We have to trust that the consultant and contractor know what they're doing. The key point is that CDs are for the contractor. (See Figure 14)

A contractor uses both equipment and personnel to translate the information in the drawings and specifications into construction activities. Construction is not a linear process, but "more resembles a network of simultaneous activities."[19] The first sheet or two of the drawing package will identify the project, project owner, all the consultants whose work is represented in the package, code requirements, legends, table of contents of the drawings, and other boiler plate information. Thereafter, the drawings follow the order of construction operations and are usually identified by an abbreviation related to the relevant discipline, as follows: (See Figure 15)

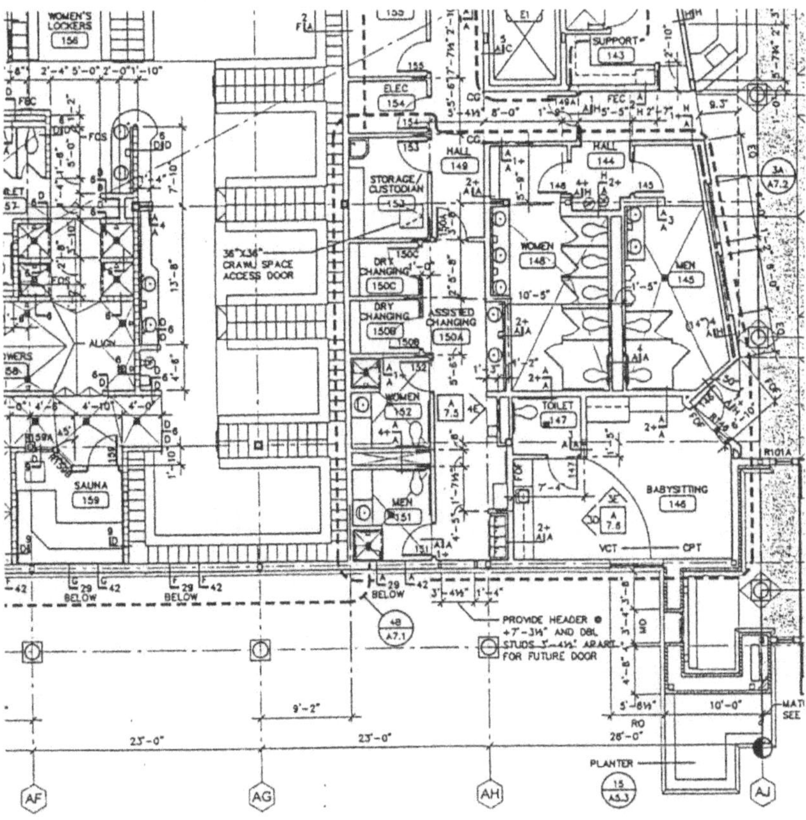

Figure 14. Construction Drawing

- **C**ivil—survey plan, existing conditions, the proposed site plan, site utilities, grading, drainage, parking, paving, and site circulation.
- **L**andscape—planting design, site furniture, other landscape elements.
- **A**rchitecture—floor plans, elevations, sections, casework, etc.
- **S**tructural—foundation plans, structural framing details, roofing details, etc.
- **M**echanical—heating, ventilation, and air-conditioning (HVAC) plans and details.
- **P**lumbing—plumbing fixtures, restroom plans, etc.
- **E**lectrical—electrical plans, power distribution, lighting, etc.

For some projects, there may be additional drawings for various specialties such as laboratory design, production kitchens and food service, interiors, signage and wayfinding, and audiovisual equipment.

Specifications

"Specifications" (more properly called Technical Specifications) usually refers to the book of written material which, with the drawings, constitutes the Contract Documents. Specifications describe in full the requirements and terms of agreement between owner and contractor. (See Figure 16) They detail the type and quality of all the materials, the standards of workman-

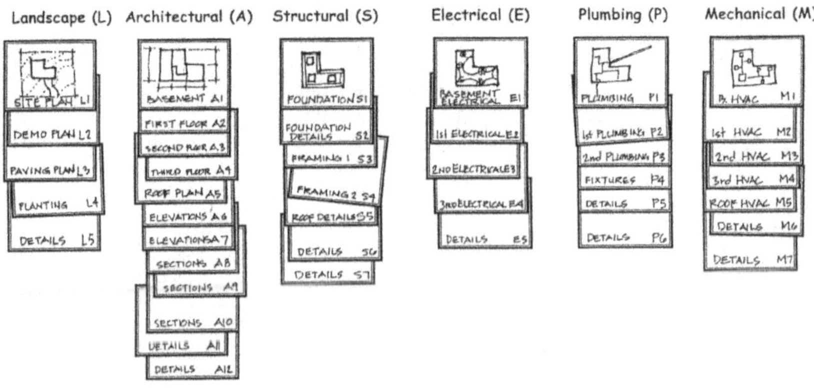

Figure 15. Sample Drawing Package

ship expected, and which trades will be responsible for which portions of the work. They're also a great cure for insomnia.

Bid Packages

Construction Documents are often divided into discrete packages that are released to contractors so they can make construc-

STUDENT RECREATION CENTER
SITE PREPARATION AND DEMOLITION PACKAGE — **16315**
UNIVERSITY OF IDAHO — **UNDERGROUND DUCTBANK**
Northwest Architectural Company, P.S. 98100 — **Page 2**

ACCEPTABLE MANUFACTURERS;

Ducts: P.W.Pipe and Carlon

Substitutions may be considered only when submitted in conformance with Section 16010.

PART 3 – EXECUTION

INSTALLATION:

Arrange ductbank as shown on the drawings. Spacers and reinforcing steel shall be rigidly secured together to prevent duct movement during concrete pour.

Sides of concrete encasement shall be made with straight forms. Trench walls will not be used concrete forms for encasement.

[Drill and embed a minimum of four #4 reinforcing steel bars into existing underground concre structures. Reinforcing steel shall be attached to existing concrete structures with epoxy grout. Steel bars shall be located at the corners of the ductbank and extend a minimum of 24" into the ductbank.]

Ducts shall run in a straight line, with only standard bends as allowed on the drawings, and graded vertically to slope to handhole. Crooked runs will not be allowed.

All joints in plastic ducts shall be cemented as recommended by the manufacturer. All ducts shall be watertight. Where it is established that ducts are not watertight, they shall be exposed and necessary corrections made. Duct runs shall be installed so that all runs slope to the associated manhole.

Provide end bells where ducts terminate in vaults or utility tunnels.

Provide non-metallic duct spacers at 5'-0" intervals, maximum spacing.

During construction, partially completed ductlines shall be protected from the entrance of debri such as mud, sand, and dirt by means of suitable conduit plugs. As each section of ductbank is completed, a testing mandrel shall be drawn through until the conduit is clear of all particles of earth, sand, or gravel. Conduit plugs shall then be immediately reinstalled.

END OF SECTION 16315

Figure 16. Sample Specification

tion estimates, i.e. "bids." These "bid packages" fall into categories such as a foundation bid package, a framing bid package, or a masonry bid package. Putting out some bid packages early can be advantageous. If the site is ready for demolition, excavation, foundations and site utilities, time can be saved by initiating these activities even before the rest of the Construction Documents are completed. An early bid package can also ensure that these operations occur under the best possible weather conditions.

Sometimes the early bid package will include all work up through the structural skeleton, i.e. the steel framing work. This can be because of steel's long delivery lead times, or because its price may be climbing and the bid package is let out to secure potential cost savings. If you know you can get it going, you can often save time and money by putting out early bid packages. But if you make any substantial design alterations after an early bid package has been let, the resulting change orders will likely offset any savings you've realized.

Final Cost Estimates

As noted before, knowledge about a project increases at each successive stage. Having gone through Schematic Design with an estimate based on rough square footage costs, and having gone through Design Development with estimates based on unit costs, we now arrive at the end of Construction Documents and a final cost estimate. At this point, nearly everything "knowable" about the project is known, the "unknowables" being things like the exact nature of underground site conditions; hidden conditions in a building that's being remodeled; precise knowledge of the bidding and construction climate, and the cost of some building materials that fluctuate with construction demand. The project budget has a 5 percent construction contingency for the express purpose of covering these "unknowables." The final cost estimates should be within plus or minus 2 to 5 percent of the established budget or the MACC (maximum allowable construction cost). If the final estimate is over the

MACC by 5 percent, or whatever your contingency amount is, the project may be in trouble. It's not unknown for a project not to go to bid because the final estimate is so far off the budget. This is where a third-party estimator is well worth the expense.

Chapter 3
Construction Administration

Once the Construction Documents (CDs) are complete and accepted and the final cost estimate is reconciled with the budget, the project enters the next stage: securing bids from contractors and, ultimately, construction. The design consultants' role at this stage is called Construction Administration, or "CA." They have a vested interest in making sure their project is well-managed and well-built, and are in the best position to answer any questions about the project as the contractor moves forward. It is important, however, to pin down exactly what they will and won't do as part of their basic service package.

SERVICES IN CONSTRUCTION ADMINISTRATION

The services that an A/E can provide in CA are divided into those provided before construction and those provided during construction.

Services provided before construction include:

- Bidding Assistance
- Contract Award
- Notice to Proceed

Services provided during construction include:

- Site Visits

- Submittal Services
- Testing and Inspection
- Change Orders
- Requests for Information
- Interpretations and Decisions
- Project Closeout

All of these potential services are described below.

SERVICES PROVIDED BEFORE CONSTRUCTION

Bidding Assistance

In order to put the CD package into the hands of qualified contractors for the purpose of bidding, the A/E provides bidding assistance to the client/owner. This can include:

- Developing separate bid packages as part of the basic services agreement
- Reproducing all of the copies necessary for bidding
- Advertising the project bid
- Answering questions from bidders
- Issuing addendums (These can be clarifications of the bid package, or expansions of the scope of work being bid. It's critical that all bidders receive all addendums—otherwise bid review will be comparing "apples and oranges.")
- Evaluating and reviewing submitted bids
- Addressing legal problems with bids
- Contract award
- Notice to the contractor to proceed

Bidding

The bid process involves soliciting construction estimates from contractors. In an ideal world, the design consultant's final estimate of construction cost would match the contractor's estimate of construction cost. (And sometimes that actually happens!) Each contractor will provide estimates of how much it will cost to construct the project as drawn and specified in the Contract

Documents. The lowest bid usually, but not always, wins the contract. If the low bidder is very low, concern is justified. The bidder probably left something out of the bid, in which case the process allows them to withdraw it. You can then award the contract to the next lowest bidder.

Several factors can influence the outcome of a bid: the time of year the bid is let (Are the contractors already busy for the year?), construction market conditions (Is the price of construction materials inflated or is the market weak?), and even the overall economy (e.g. interest rates). In order to protect the owner and the project from the vagaries of the construction market, the bid is sometimes broken up into separate "bid packages."

The Base Bid

Even when the document package is divided into "bid packages," the main bid package is called the "base bid." In a volatile bidding climate, or in cases where additional funding might become available, the bid package may include "add alternates" or "deduct alternates," which serve as "bid protection."

Add Alternates are project components desired by the owner but not included in the base bid. If the bids are lower than the budget, these alternative items can be added to the bid proposal. (One caution here: make sure that your base bid is really the base building you need! If there are components that must be included for successful functioning of the facility, they should be in the base bid, not in an add alternate.) A typical Add Alternate would be to upgrade levels or quality of finishes. For example, the base bid may include tile floors in offices but the Add Alternate may be for carpeting, which would only be included if there were room in the budget to meet both the base bid and the add alternate amount.

Deduct Alternates are project components desired by the owner that could be removed if the bids are higher than the budget. This provides "bid protection," and can allow the project to move forward, even in difficult bidding conditions. If, for example, the base bid included carpet in all offices, the deduct alternate might be for tile, in order to lower the bid by the difference in cost between the two.

Contract Award

The contract for construction services is awarded to the apparent low bidder, generally in the form of an official letter from the client to the contractor. The award usually can't be made until all kinds of legal steps are followed (e.g. verification of business licenses and insurance) and any possible challenges to the bid are addressed to the satisfaction of all bidders. Be forewarned: on a larger project or in a tight market, unsuccessful bidders are likely to contest the award to the winning contractor, often on the basis of a technicality. (Sometimes contractors have long histories of ill will toward each other and your project becomes another forum for their ongoing dispute.)

Notice to Proceed

The official "Notice to Proceed" is also known as the "NTP." It's another official letter (after the Contract Award Letter) from the client to the contractor, indicating acceptance and approval of the contractor's bid. It provides official notification to proceed with construction and usually stipulates both start and finish dates for the project.

SERVICES PROVIDED DURING CONSTRUCTION

Site Visits

How many times during the course of construction do you want your A/E to visit the project, inspect the site, and meet with owner's representatives or the contractor? There should be a minimum of one site visit a month. On larger or more complex projects, it's not uncommon for the A/E firm to have a representative on site for the duration of the project. The frequency of site visits depends on how far the project site is from the firm's office, whether the institution or agency has in-house A/E staff to manage the project, the project's scale and complexity (the more complex the project, the more frequent should be the site visits), and whether the owner has contracted for third-party Construction Management services. If the owner has a CM on site, the need for A/E site visits is greatly reduced.

Submittal Services

Often the construction specifications will call out "use product 'X' or an approved equal." Who approves the equal? Usually it's the client, but the architect often reviews it first for compliance with the design intent. Reviewing submittals can be a time-consuming process, but it can have a significant impact on the level and quality of finish on a project, so it's best left to the A/E to handle.

Testing and Inspection

This includes things like measuring the quality of steel used in the project, inspecting pipe joints, and concrete slump testing. Some of these tests are required by the state or local jurisdictions. Others are done, either by the A/E or, most often, a consultant hired for the purpose, to ensure that the project is being well built.

Change Orders

A Change Order, also known as a "CO," is written authorization from a building owner or the owner's agent to a contractor to change the scope of work, the design, the materials used, or the equipment installed on a project. The contractor, the owner, or even the A/E can initiate a Change Order. Change Orders to the scope of a project mean the cost will go up. (I've even seen a CO whose purpose was to reduce the scope of a project actually increase its cost!) Most contractors will be fair when dealing with Change Orders, but some have been known to bid low to secure a project, then depend on Change Orders to generate their profit. One question that should be asked in pre-qualifying contractors is the average number of Change Orders on their previous projects. Beware of contractors who make a lot of money this way!

There are two principal ways to avoid COs. One is thorough planning at the Pre-Design stage. If the project scope and budget are thoroughly identified, it is less likely there will be scope changes later. The other is thorough, high-quality Construction Documents, and the responsibility for this rests squarely on the shoulders of the A/E. Discrepancies between various aspects of the construction document package must be kept to an absolute minimum.

Sometimes Change Orders are unavoidable. A late donation to a project can allow scope changes, or upgrades in levels of finish or quality of materials. Advances in technology between the initial stages of a project and actual construction could necessitate a Change Order, as could fluctuations in the availability of materials, labor, contractors, etc.

Requests for Information

A Request for Information, also known as an "RFI," is usually a question from the contractor to the consultant seeking clarification and better understanding of some provision in the contract documents. It's vital that the A/E respond quickly, because delaying the contractor's progress can result in a Change Order. This is why consultants are often asked during their interview about their performance on RFIs. Ideally, no more than 24 hours should pass between issuance of the RFI and the A/E's response.

Interpretations and Decisions

If there are discrepancies between different parts of the Construction Documents or between the documents and the actual constructed product, the A/E is often in the best position to sort through these issues.

Project Closeout

Like the last few minutes of a football game, finishing a project can seem to take forever. Some of the final steps are:

- The "**Punch List**" itemizes jobs that must be completed or issues that must be resolved by the contractor before substantial completion can be declared by the contractor and accepted by the owner. It is prepared by the responsible A/E for the project, and can include tasks as minimal as touching up the paint on a wall or as major as troubleshooting why an entire HVAC system isn't working as designed. Depending on the quality of work by the contractor and the A/E's eye for detail, a punch list can be anywhere from one to 50 pages.
- **Testing** is the verification that all systems in the building—especially life safety systems—are working as designed. For instance, do elevators stop flush at each floor level, or do they need to be adjusted? Are all locking doors keyed appropriately? Does all panic hardware on emergency exits function properly? Does the fire alarm work?
- **Occupancy.** When does the Owner become the Occupant? Deciding when to occupy a "completed" building is an important step in the Construction Administration process. Some parts of a building may be ready for occupancy before the rest of it is completed, or a building may be completely operable except for a few life safety systems. It's important for your agency or institution to define, at least for the current project, what the requirements for occupancy are and how they will be met. Those requirements should include:
  - Life safety alarms
  - Smoke detection systems
  - Fire sprinkler systems
  - Magnetic hold-opens on doors
  - Elevator cut outs
  - Room numbers and other wayfinding signage (can a fireman find his way to the fire?)
  - Security cameras and alarms
  - Cardlocks or other special locks and security arrangements

Decisions about Furnishings, Fixtures, and Equipment (FF&E) are also part of occupancy. If FF&E are moved from an existing facility to the new one, who pays for it? Who schedules it? Who assigns offices, rooms, and spaces? Special care must be taken in transporting sensitive scientific or technical equipment. Warranties on such equipment are often voided if they are moved by anyone other than a manufacturer's representative. All of these decisions and questions must be resolved for a successful completion of the facility. If institutional staffing cannot handle this stage, the A/E consultant has the requisite problem-solving and project management skills to manage it. Just make sure it is a service included in the Construction Administration stage of the contract.

Final payments are made to the contractor only upon completion of all punch list items, when substantial completion has been accepted and the facility is approved for occupancy. It is not uncommon to hold a "retainage" (usually no more than 5 percent) of the contractor's billed amount to ensure full completion of the project prior to final payment.

After substantial completion has been declared, after the punch list has been completed and occupancy is permitted, comes the "move-in." This is sometimes covered by the project budget, but more often paid out of user groups' operational budgets. Next comes the official opening and building dedication, which is rarely covered by the project budget.

CONSTRUCTION DELIVERY METHODOLOGIES

Introduction

Although actual construction is nearly the last stage of a project, choosing a construction delivery method should be one of the first decisions, since some of them come into play and require planning as early as the Pre-Design phase.

For a century or more, the "Design/Bid/Build" method was used for most campus construction, but in an effort to build "better, faster, cheaper," a number of alternatives have been developed in the last 30 years. There is no "right" or "wrong" way to deliver a project. Each has its advantages and disadvantages, and the method to be used depends on the need of the agency or institution and what is best for the project. Some are better suited to alternative methods.

The four main ways a project can be delivered are:

- Design/Bid/Build (D/B/B)
- Design/Build (D/B)
- Construction Manager (CM)
- Construction Manager/General Contractor (CM/GC)

Design/Bid/Build

Design/Bid/Build is the traditional way of delivering projects. The Owner initiates the project, then the A/E consultant moves it through Pre-Design, Design Development, and construction drawings. After the design is finished and the construction documents are completed, the Owner (with assistance from the A/E) puts it out to bid for qualified contractors. The General Contractor who is awarded the contract to build the facility often subcontracts aspects of the project to specialty contractors. It's a straightforward, clean, but fairly linear process. (See Figure 17)

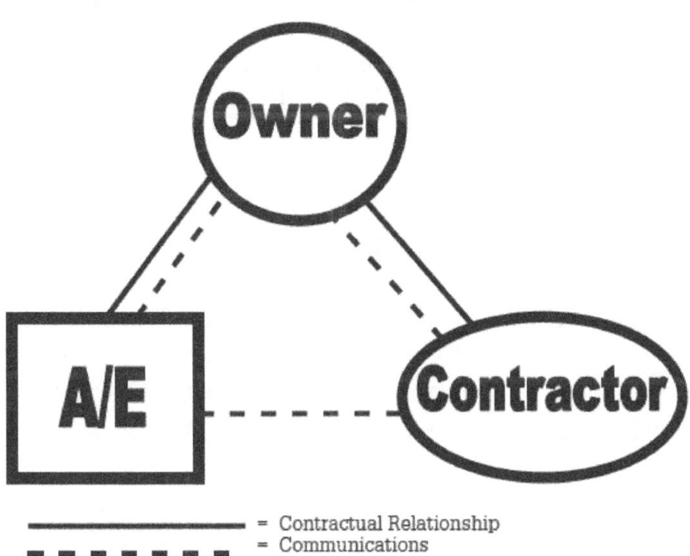

Figure 17. Design / Bid / Build

Advantages:

- Easiest process for Owners to manage
- Owners have more control over the whole process.
- Owners can participate in design.
- Because it's a common method, everyone knows his or her role.
- The end product is well defined before construction: the Owners know exactly what they're going to get.
- The A/E may be more involved in the construction phase and can function as an independent advisor to the Owner.

Disadvantages:

- Takes longer because it's a linear process
- Division of roles between the A/E and the Contractor sometimes impedes communication regarding constructability issues. (The Contractor doesn't see the design documents until bid time, where in other methods described below, the Contractor often sees the design right from the beginning and can provide constructability analysis in the early stages of the project, which is extremely beneficial.)
- Change orders are more likely.
- Higher potential for conflict between all three parties than in other methods
- The Owner can be caught in the middle of disputes between the A/E and the Contractor.

Design/Build

In this method, the same consulting firm does both the design and the construction. Thus, the Owner deals with a single point of responsibility for all aspects of the project. The D/B entity assumes all responsibility to the Owner for the cost, schedule, and quality of the product. Owners can focus their efforts on defining the scope and needs of the project rather than on coordination between the designer and the builder.

A study by Mark Konchar and Victor Sanvido of Pennsylvania State University that compared the cost, schedule, and quality of 351 projects nationwide showed that, on average, projects using

Design/Build took 33.5 percent less time to deliver and had a 6.1 percent lower unit cost than similar projects delivered in a traditional manner.[20]

There are several variations on the D/B method. The designer may hire a contractor to build the project, or the contractor may serve as the lead consultant and hire an A/E to provide the design, or it may be a joint venture to design and construct as a single entity. Few construction firms have architects or engineers on staff; D/Bs are usually marriages of convenience where the parties come together for a specific project and split up when it's done.

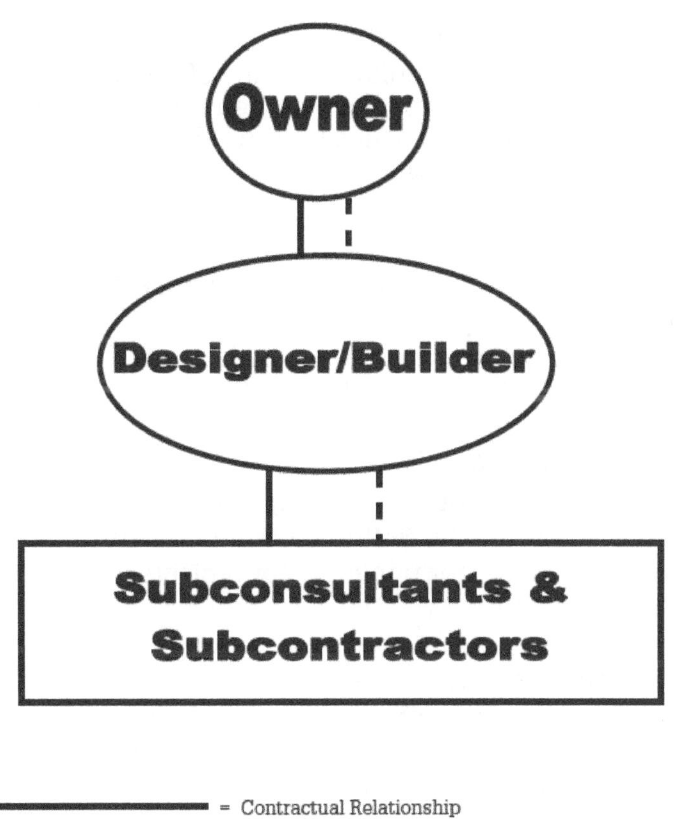

Figure 18. Design / Build

Another variation of the Design/Build method is "bridging," in which an independent A/E is hired to be the Owner's bridging consultant, defining a program through Pre-Design and representing the Owner on the project. The Owner uses the Pre-Design products prepared by the bridging consultant to solicit bids from D/B firms. The D/B firm then develops the project from there. (See Figure 18)

Advantages:

- Single point of responsibility in the design and delivery process
- Potential for the fastest delivery
- Best suited for conventional projects that have no special technical requirements
- Project costs may be lower.
- Simplified dispute resolution; many of the normal conflicts that occur in a project (e.g. between designer and contractor) become internal issues for the D/B team that the Owner never has to deal with.

Disadvantages:

- The A/E cannot function as an independent advisor to the owner.
- Depending on how the Design/Build team is led, the Owner may lose contact with part of the team.
- The drive to cut costs can erode the quality of both design and construction.
- Can be problematic for highly specialized projects, or projects with significant high-tech requirements
- May not be legal for public sector projects in some jurisdictions.

Construction Manager

The Construction Manager method, also known as "Agency Construction Management," has been called "a concept in search of a definition," since there are so many ways to define and use it. The CM's responsibilities can vary widely from project to project and run the gamut from Pre-Design to post-construction. They are, in fact, most effective when engaged in a project from its inception. A CM serves as the Owner's representative and can offer services that include cost estimating, constructability review and analysis, value engineering, bid assistance, commissioning, and construction oversight. The CM will administer the contracts, keep track of the work, the payments, the change orders, and the RFIs, etc. Since CMs furnish neither materials nor labor and no cash flows through the their books, they have no financial interest in the project. The CM usually offers no guarantees about schedule, cost, or quality of construction . . . although some will guarantee that they'll save you at least the amount of their fee. (See Figure 19)

Advantages:

- Easy for the Owner to manage.

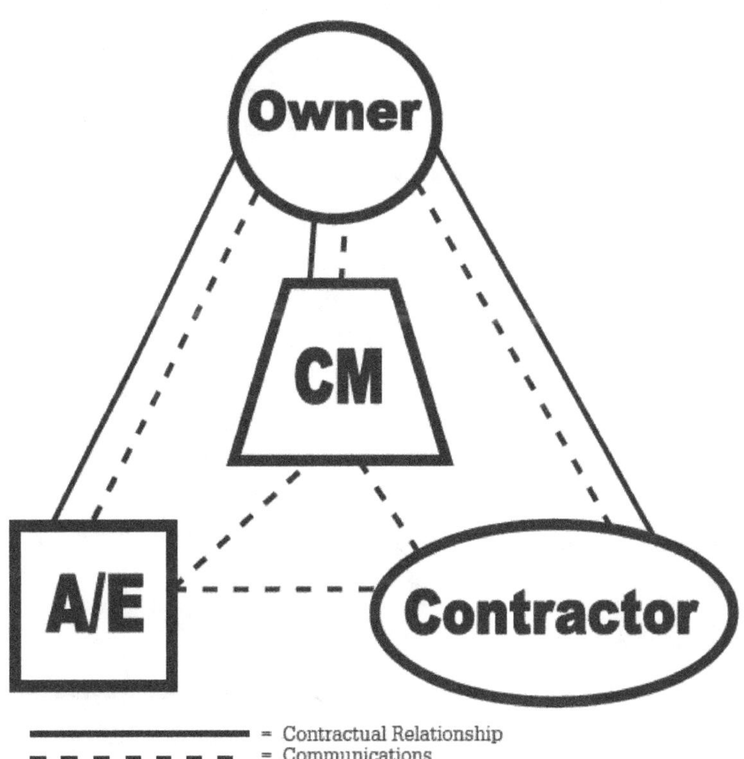

Figure 19. Construction Manager

- Good to use when the Owner doesn't have the in-house staff or knowledge to oversee the project
- Good to use when the project is especially complex or requires extensive coordination
- Can be very fast when design and construction are managed concurrently

Disadvantages:

- May cost more due to third-party involvement by the CM, although this could be offset by savings the CM generates.
- May require extra time for selecting, defining scope, negotiating, and contracting with CM
- Introducing another party into the mix increases the potential for disputes between the Owner, CM, A/E, and Contractor.

Construction Manager/General Contractor

In CM/GC, the Construction Manager (CM) also acts as the General Contractor (GC). Many states have mandated this method, also called GC/CM or Construction Management At Risk (CMAR), for state agencies and public higher education institu-

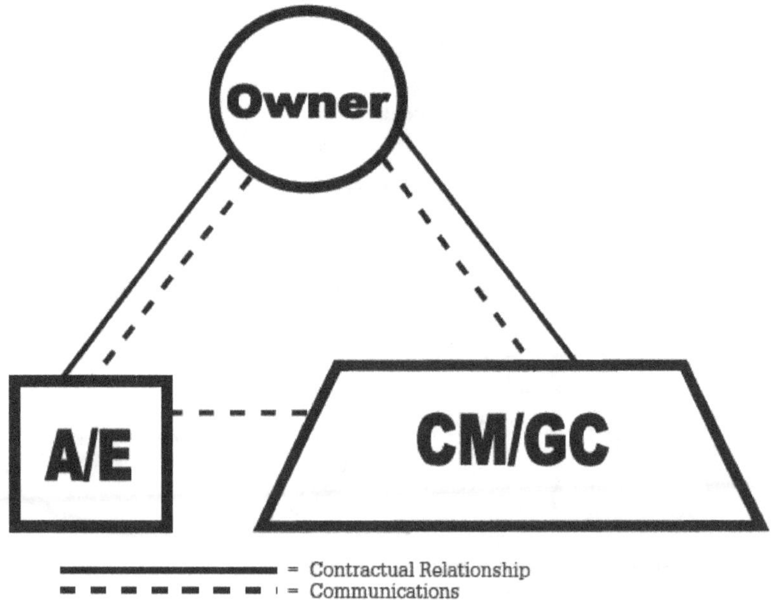

Figure 19. Construction Manager/General Contractor

tions. Acting as the General Contractor, the Construction Manager takes on all responsibilities associated with construction and management of the project, including contracting with subcontractors, ordering materials and equipment, ensuring job safety, taking care of permits and bids, and meeting schedules. A significant feature of this method is that the CM/GC provides a "guaranteed maximum price" or GMP, either at the end of Design Development or at some percentage (often 85 percent) of completion of the Construction Documents. "At Risk" means that if the cost of the project exceeds the GMP, the CMAR pays the difference. If the project comes in under budget, the CMAR gets to keep part or all of the difference. Obviously, this gives the contractor a powerful incentive to keep costs down and meet the schedule. (See Figure 20)

Advantages:

- Good to use when the Owner doesn't have the staff or knowledge to oversee the project
- Good to use when the project is especially complex or requires extensive coordination
- Can be very fast when design and construction are managed concurrently; even before the design is entirely finished, the CM/GC can bid and subcontract those portions of it that are complete.
- A guaranteed maximum price, the value of which should not be underestimated
- The CM (rather than the Owner) is at risk for cost overruns, delays, and estimate (or GMP) compliance.

Disadvantages:

- Not the easiest process for the Owner to manage
- The GMP is rarely lower and often higher than the cost of other methods. (That's the price of certainty!)
- May cost more due to third-party involvement by the CMAR, although this could be offset by savings the CMAR generates.
- Selecting, defining scope, negotiating, and contracting with CMAR may require extra time.

- May create adversarial relationships and disputes between the CMAR, the A/E, and/or subcontractors due to pressure on the CMAR to meet budget and schedule requirements.

Final Thoughts on Construction Delivery

Assuming you are not required by state law or institutional policy to use a particular delivery method, there are several questions to consider in choosing one. Does your institution have in-house design and project management staff capable of managing every stage of a capital project? If so, do they have experience with the kind of project you're undertaking? Is the project relatively simple, such as office space or classrooms, or complex, such as high-tech laboratories? (Remember that a small project can be complex because of its staging, location, schedule, or user group, while a physically large project can be simple to construct). Are you on a tight schedule? If so, methods that allow fast-tracking and beginning construction before design is complete should be considered. If not, a traditional method that provides the best economic value might be preferable. The delivery method to use is the one that best aligns with the size, complexity, and schedule of the project.

BUILDING COMMISSIONING

The advent of computer-controlled, high-tech HVAC and other building systems has made it increasingly important to coordinate all of a facility's systems with each other. This is especially true of laboratory facilities, where it's not unusual for more than 50 percent of the construction cost to be invested in the HVAC system. Building commissioning is the term for the systematic process of achieving, ensuring, and verifying that all building systems perform interactively according to the documented design intent and the owner's operational needs. This process often begins in the design phase of a project, continues through all subsequent stages, sometimes lasts for a year after project close-out, and includes the training of maintenance and operating staff.[21]

A Commissioning Agent is the person who performs commissioning on all the building systems from design through construction. The Commissioning Agent is most often a mechanical engineer, but can be anyone with extensive knowledge of construction and general building systems, especially HVAC systems.

There are at least three ways to deliver commissioning services:

- Agency Commissioning
- Contractor Commissioning
- Third-Party Commissioning

"Better is the end of a thing than the beginning thereof. . ."
—Ecclesiastes 7:8

Agency Commissioning is when the commissioning agent is a direct employee of the Owner, agency, or institution. It's sometimes called Owner Commissioning. The advantage is that the agent will know your systems, your institution, your priorities, your staff's capabilities, and what you can live with and what you can't. It also doesn't add any cost to the project, since the agent is already an employee of the Owner. The disadvantage is that this individual has to take time from other responsibilities to handle commissioning.

Contractor Commissioning is when the Contractor building the facility also performs commissioning services. This service is offered by some larger contractors as they supervise the work of subconsultants. Some have suggested that this is like having the fox guard the hen house. But who is better equipped or in a better position than the Contractor to ensure that everything works and that all systems are integrated and coordinated? It makes a lot of sense in some ways, but it is also fraught with potential for serious conflicts of interest.

Third-Party Commissioning is when the Owner hires an independent consultant to do the commissioning and interact with the

Contractor throughout the process. Third-party commissioning agents provide tremendous expertise and (theoretically) an objective point of view. They also increase the cost of construction by one or two percent, which may sound like a lot until you consider the cost over its lifetime of a building that never quite works as planned.

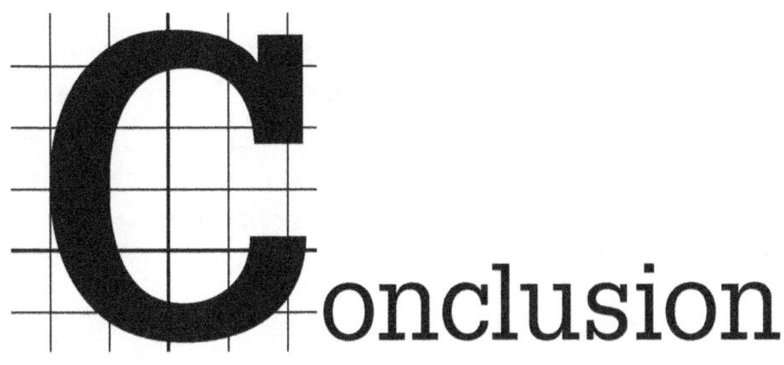

Conclusion

It's said that good judgment comes from experience, and experience comes from bad judgment. Or, put another way by Mark Twain, "A man who carries a cat by the tail learns something he can learn in no other way." This is certainly true for major capital projects. I hope that my experience, paltry as it is (and having its genesis in bad judgment), will provide help and insight for you as you are called upon to take a role in such a project. I still believe that there is little in life as satisfying or as pleasurable as successfully completing a major project and knowing you positively influenced the outcome. I love to go back and visit buildings I have been involved in, knowing that a wall, window, view, or space is there because I spoke up. It is gratifying to see a building or space functioning exactly as I had envisioned it. It makes all the stress, frustration, and effort seem worthwhile. I hope that is your experience as well.

"A man who carries a cat by the tail learns something he can learn in no other way."

—Mark Twain

ENDNOTES

1 By "capital project," I mean the design and construction of a new building or a major remodel of an existing facility. Most state governments and educational institutions define "capital" in the economic sense: something tangible (like land or a building) used as a means for production. By "major" I mean a cost in excess of $2 million, but its definition varies from state to state.

2 Stewart Brand, *How Buildings Learn* (New York: Viking, 1994), p. 3.

3 This listing defines the process from an architect's frame of reference. John Holcomb, writing from an educational administrator's point of view in his book *A Guide to Planning Educational Facilities* (3rd Edition, 1995, University Press of America), identifies eight steps: (1) Thinking and Needs Assessment; (2) Planning and Commitment; (3) Design; (4) "Selling"; (5) Financing; (6) Construction; (7) Occupation and In-Service Orientation; and (8) Evaluation.

4 This stage is also sometimes referred to as "Programming," which is more accurately understood as one part of the Pre-Design stage. An architectural "program" is a product of Pre-Design, but it is not all of Pre-Design.

5 For an excellent article on this subject, see "Pre-Design Planning" by Ksenia J. Merck and William F. Merck in *From Concept to Commissioning*, edited by Donald Guckert and published by APPA (The Assocation of Higher Education Facilities Officers) in 2002.

6 Rush, s. & Johnson, S. (1989). *The Decaying American Campus: A Ticking Time Bomb.* Alexandria, VA: Association of Higher Education Facilities Officers & National Association of College and University Business Officers.

7 Roger L. Brauer, *Facilities Planning: The User Requirements Method* (New York: American Management Association, 1986), p. 161.

8 William Pena. *Problem Seeking: An Architectural Programming Primer* (Washington, D.C.: AIA Press, 1987) p. 15.

9 Donna Duerk. Architectural Programming: Information Management for Design (New York: Van Nostrand Reinhold, 1993) p. 8.

10 Pena, *Problem Seeking*, p 18.

11 Lee Ingalls, Barbara V. Bruxvoort, and Jason Mihos, eds., *Facilities Planning Handbook, 3rd Edition* (Orinda, California: Tradeline, Inc., 1995), p. 339.

12 ibid, p. 361.

13 This is a very general rule of thumb and varies significantly with building type and project size.

14 This number is purely for illustration. Readers should not assume that any particular project could be built for this amount. I've seen projects built for less than this and I've seen projects built for three times this amount.

15 Ray McClure, "Choosing Your Team," *American School & University*, November 1, 2002; Accessed online at http://asumag.com/mag/university_choosing_team/index.html, August 6, 2004.

16 This glossary of terms is available online at www.asu.edu/aad/manuals/cpm/cpm002.html
Another valuable glossary can also be accessed online at www.pmforum.org/library/glossary/index.htm

17 www.asu.edu/aad/manuals/cpm/cpm002.html

18 Edward Allen, *How Buildings Work* [need publication info], p. 209.

19 Time Saver Standards for Landscape Architecture (New York: McGraw-Hill, 1998), pp. 110-112.

20 Ray McClure, "Choosing Your Team," American School and University, November 1, 2002; Accessed online at http://asumag.com/mag/university_choosing_team/index.html, August 6, 2004

21 Nancy Benner and Carolyn Dasher, "Commissioning: Adding Value to Your Business," presented at The Northwest Conference on Building Commissioning, 1996. Accessed online at http://www.teamkd.com/build-services/bldg-comm.html#, August 6, 2004

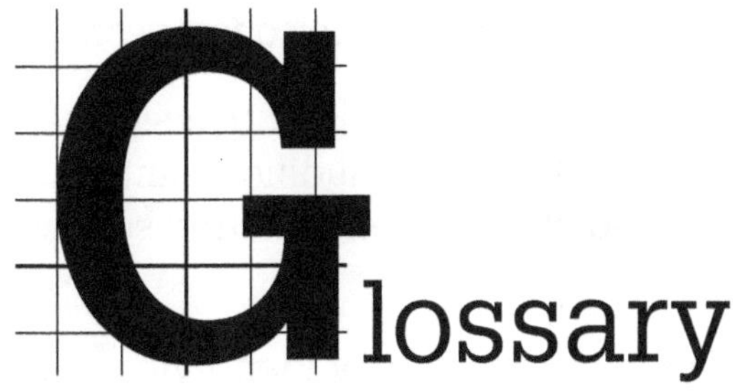

Glossary

A number in parentheses following a term refers to the list of sources which follows the glossary, identifying the source from which the definition was derived.

Words or terms that appear in **bold face** in definitions also have their own entries in the glossary.

Add Alternate - Project components desired by the Owner but not included in the **base bid**. If the bids are lower than the budget, these alternative items can be added to the bid proposal.

Additional Services - Services provided by an **A/E** consultant that are not included in "Basic Services."

A/E - The abbreviation for Architect/Engineer consultant.

AIA - The abbreviation for the American Institute of Architects.

As-Built Drawings (8) - The revised drawings which truly reflect what was constructed, including field verification. Not usually included in **Basic Services** by the **A/E** unless specifically requested and negotiated for by the Owner.

Base Bid - The competitive bid proposed by a contractor for the base **bid package** of a project. The apparent low base bid is not necessarily accepted until an analysis of **add alternates** and **deduct alternates** are included in the comparison.

Basic Services - Those essential programming and design services provided by an **A/E** consultant, including architectural, structural, mechanical, and electrical engineering services for a project.

Benchmarking - An ongoing methodology for identifying, measuring, and comparing processes, facilities, or policies.

Bid Assistance - Assistance provided by an **A/E** to the Owner to procure, review, evaluate, and negotiate proposed bids

Bid Package - The sorting of the construction/bidding documents and process into discrete units, e.g. foundation bid package, framing bid package, masonry bid package. Sometimes bid packages are chronologically divided, i.e. an "early" bid package and a "late" bid package.

Bid Protection - Using **add alternates** or **deduct alternates** in the **bid package** to cover the vagaries of the bidding climate.

Bidding - Collecting competitive cost proposals from contractors.

Budget Creep - A guy in the budget office who gives everyone the willies. Seriously, it's the incremental budget growth that occurs as a result of **Design Creep**. Budget Creep usually takes the form of budget demand with little or no budget reality to support it.

Building Costs - The actual costs of constructing a building; usually includes all costs of construction within five feet of the building line as well as all items necessary to make the building habitable by code, e.g. fire extinguishers, sprinkler systems, alarms, etc. Building costs are part of the **Construction Budget**, which also includes **Fixed Equipment** and **Site Development**.

Building Efficiency Ratio - The ratio of **Net Square Feet** to **Gross Square Feet**. Often expressed as a percentage. The formula is: **NSF/GSF** x 100 = Building Efficiency

CA - The abbreviation for **Construction Administration**.

Capital Project - Technically, any physical asset or resource that benefits a program for more than a year (definitions vary from state to state). These can include land, buildings, improvements and additions to buildings, equipment and library books. For the purposes of this book, capital projects are buildings and site developments that surround them.

Casework - The built-in cabinets, shelving, and counters that are part of a project. Usually included in the **Building Cost** as **Fixed Equipment**.

CD - The abbreviation for **Construction Documents**.

Change Order (1) - Written authorization from a building Owner or the Owner's agent to a contractor to change the scope of work, design, materials used, or equipment installed. Also known as **C.O.** Generally speaking, the fewer the C.O.s a project experiences, the better.

Chiller (7) - The piece of **HVAC** equipment that chills the water used to cool a building. Chillers are fueled by electricity, gas, or steam. Because they produce vibration, heat, and noise, chillers should be located as far as possible from spaces whose use would be disrputed by them.

CIP Concrete - "Cast-in-place" concrete.

Circular Definition - See **Definition, Circular**.

Clerk of the Works - Someone who represents the Owner on site during construction, similar to an Owner's **Construction Manager**. The Clerk of the Works expedites **RFIs** and **COs**. Also known as an "On-Site Representative."

CM -The abbreviation for **Construction Management** or **Construction Manager**.

CMAR - The abbreviation for **Construction Manager At Risk**

CM/GC - The abbreviation for **Construction Manager/General Contractor.** See also **GC/CM**.

CMU - The abbreviation for Concrete Masonry Unit, concrete blocks used in construction.

CO - The abbreviation for **Change Order**.

Commissioning - The process for achieving, verifying, and documenting that the performance of a building and its systems meets design intent as well as the Owner and occupant's operational needs. The process extends through all phases of a project, from initial concept to occupancy and operation, and includes the training of maintenance personnel.

Construction Administration - The administration by the Owner or Owner's agent of the construction phase of a capital project.

Construction Budget - A portion (usually around 65%) of a **Project Budget** that includes **Building Cost**, **Fixed Equipment**, and **Site Development**.

Construction Documents (3) - The drawings and specifications that are the legal contract for the accurate production of a building project, including site work, landscaping, interiors, equipment, and all building systems.

Construction Manager (2) - A broad term covering a variety of project delivery scenarios in which a construction manager is added to the building team to oversee scheduling, cost control, constructibility, project management, bidding or negotiating construction contracts, and construction.

Contingency - A line item and amount in a budget to cover unanticipated expenses that will occur during a project. Project budgets often include contingencies to cover both construction and non-construction-related items.

Contract Documents - see **Construction Documents**.

DD - The abbreviation for **Design Development**.

Deduct Alternates - Project components that are desired by the Owner but could be removed from the **base bid** if the bids exceed the budget.

Definition, Circular - See **Circular Definition**.

Design Concept(s) (6)- An idea for a physical solution to a client/Owner's architectural problem. A design concept is a proposed response to a **Program Concept**.

Design Creep - A sleazy architect. Not really, just kidding. Actually, it is the expansion of project scope that often occurs through the design phase of a project. "Terminal" Design Creep will kill a project. The degree of Design Creep a project experiences is inversely proportional to the quantity and quality of effort expended in **Pre-Design** and **Programming** phases.

Design Development - The second stage of the project process (following Schematic Design) wherein an alternative **Design Concept** has been selected and a more specific, detailed design is developed.

Design-Bid-Build (2) - The traditional method of project delivery, in which the Owner commissions an architect or engineer to prepare drawings and specifications under a design services contract, which are put out to bid, after which the Owner separately contracts with a contractor for construction.

Design-Build (2) - A project delivery method in which the client contracts with a single entity to provide both design and construction services. The design-build entity may be a single firm, a consortium, or a joint venture assembled for the project.

Facility Study - A narrowly focused **Feasibility Study** aimed specifically at a physical facility solution to an Owner's problem.

Fast Track (2) - A process in which certain design portions of an **A/E**'s professional services overlap with construction activities in order to expedite the Owner's completion or occupancy of the project.

Feasibility Study (9)- A study performed to determine if a project is financially, physically, and legally possible.

FF&E - The abbreviation for **Furnishings, Fixtures, and Equipment.**

Free Lunch - No definition available. Popular opinion is right for once: there is no such thing.

Furnishings, Fixtures, and Equipment - The furnishings, blinds, carpets, shelves, (sometimes) casework, movable lighting, and other equipment that is not hard-wired or hard-plumbed into a building.

GC/CM - The abbreviation for General Contractor/Construction Manager.

General Contractor - The main or **Prime Contractor** who prepares bids for Owner review and also holds subcontractors' contracts.

GMP - The abbreviation for **Guaranteed Maximum Price**.

Gross Square Feet (1) - All of the floor space inside a building, measured from the outside surfaces of exterior walls. Also, the result of wearing ugly square-toed shoes that are too tight.

GSF - The abbreviation for **Gross Square Feet**.

Guaranteed Maximum Price - The price of construction guaranteed by a **CM**, **CMAR**, **CM/GC** or **GC/CM**.

Guidelines, Design - A university or agency's general principles to guide design. They differ from **Standards** in that guidelines are more aspirational and descriptive rather than prescriptive.

HVAC - The abbreviation for Heating, Ventilation, Air-Conditioning, the mechanical systems of a building.

Life Cycle Cost (1) - The sum of initial costs and operating, maintenance and replacement costs, less salvage value, over the life of a facility.

Material Testing - The verification of the quality and quantity of materials used in construction, usually performed by a third-party testing firm under the supervision of the architect or Owner.

NASF - The abbreviation for **Net Assignable Square Feet**

Net Assignable Square Feet - The **Net Square Feet** that can be specifically assigned to users.

Net Square Feet (1) - The net floor space in a building measured from the inside surfaces of exterior walls and excluding interior walls, partitions, mechanical equipment rooms, lavatories, janitorial closets, elevators, stairways, major circulation corridors, aisles, and elevator lobbies.

Notice to Proceed - The official notification by the Owner to a consultant or contractor that work on the project can begin.

NSF - The abbreviation for **Net Square Feet**.

NTP - Abbreviation for **Notice to Proceed**

Owner - Often confused with "user" or "client," the "**Owner**" is the entity that will officially own and/or operate a completed capital project. For public institutions, the legal "Owner" is the board of trustees or regents who represent the state government, even though they may never set foot in the building. It's the institution itself that will use and operate it. Obviously, this can create a difficult situation for the A/E consultant, whose check is signed by the Owner but who receives instructions and demands mostly from the users.

Owner's Budget - That portion of a **Project Budget** controlled by the Owner (institution or agency), usually comprising all overhead expenses related to the delivery of the project except the **Construction Budget**. Overhead expenses include, but are not limited to, **A/E** fees, land costs, **FFE**, and **Contingencies**.

Planning - In terms of a capital project, it is a process (mistakenly assumed to be rational) that identifies a need and the alternatives for meeting it, then determines a direction to pursue toward solutions.

Post-Occupancy Evaluation (3) - Evaluations that focus on the satisfaction and behavior of a project's **Users**.

Pre-Design (3) - The phase of a project where the services provided by an **A/E** could include feasibility studies, master planning, programming, the conceptual stage of design, and research for a design project. See also **Planning** and **Programming**.

Prime Consultant - The consultant, most often an architect, who takes the lead on a project team. Depending on the type of project, the prime consultant could also be a landscape architect or an engineer. Often called the "Architect of Record."

Prime Contractor - Also know as the **General Contractor** that holds the contracts of subcontractors.

Principal Architect - Usually the highest-ranking member of the **A/E** firm on the design team. Often the individual responsible for all major design decisions. See also **Project Architect** and **Project Manager**.

Professional Fees - Monetary compensation for **A/E** consultants.

Programmatic Concepts (6) - Ideas intended mainly as functional and organizational solutions to the client or Owner's performance problems.

Programming (8) - The process necessary to define the scope of a project, conduct master planning for future work, or delineate existing conditions. See also **Planning** and **Pre-Design**

Project Architect - The architectural consultant responsible for managing the design effort on a project. See also **Principal Architect** and **Project Manager**

Project Budget - The total budget required to build and occupy a facility, composed of the **Construction Budget** and the **Owner's Budget.**

Project Manager - The individual from the **A/E** firm responsible for organizing, directing, managing, and controlling the activities of the entire consultant team (including the Owner). This is the key individual in a project. The Owner, agency, or institution often has its own project management staff who perform the same functions but from the Owner's point of view. Never underestimate the importance of this individual in determining how smoothly and successfully a project is delivered.

Proposal(s) - The submittal prepared by an **A/E** firm in response to an Owner's **Request for Proposals**.

Proprietary Specification (1) - When an Owner or architect specifies a particular brand of equipment or technique in the construction documents. A proprietary specification prohibits the contractor from using any other brand or manufacturer's product. Proprietary specifications are usually included for good reasons, but tend to drive up costs by eliminating competition.

Punch List - The **punch list** itemizes jobs that must be completed or issues that must be resolved by the contractor before substantial completion can be declared by the contractor and accepted by the owner. It is prepared by the responsible A/E for the project, and can include tasks as minimal as touching up the paint on a wall or as major as troubleshooting why an entire HVAC system isn't working as designed.

Record Drawings - See **As-Built Drawings**.

Request for Proposals - A solicitation issued by an Owner, agency or institution for proposals from interested **A/E** consultants. Often called a Request for Qualifications or **RFQ**.

Request for Information - A request from a contractor to the architect or Owner for a clarification of intent or understanding in the **Construction Documents**. Also known as an **RFI**. Failing to respond quickly to an **RFI** can delay the project.

Retainage (1) - A portion of the money earned by the contractor that is withheld from periodic payments and retained by the Owner as assurance that the contractor will complete the project. Contractors sometimes view this as a form of blackmail.

RFI - The abbreviation for **Request for Information**.

RFQ - Request for Qualifications. See **Request for Proposals**.

Schematic Design (3) - The first stage of the design process. Using the program as a base, alternative solutions are developed. General, broad-brush decisions are made at this stage.

SD - The abbreviation for **Schematic Design**.

Site Development - The planning, design, and construction of the area immediately outside of a building, which can include landscaping, parking, plazas, courtyards, sidewalks, etc. Usually defined as the area more than five feet from the exterior walls of a building.

SOQ - The abbreviation for **Statement of Qualifications**.

Special Services - The design, administrative, or management services provided by an **A/E** or other sub-consultant that are not included in **Basic Services**. See also **Additional Services**.

Specifications (1) - Usually refers to the book of written material that, along with the drawings, constitute the **Contract Documents**, describing in full the requirements and terms of agreement between Owner and contractor. More properly called "Technical Specifications."

Standards, Design - An agency or institution's minimum requirements in design. While **Guidelines** are aspirational and descriptive, standards are prescriptive, specifying the methods, processes, brands, and products required by the Owner.

Statement of Qualifications - The submittal prepared by an **A/E** firm in response to an Owner's **Request for Proposals** or Request for Qualifications. Also known as an **SOQ**.

Sub-consultant - A consultant who contracts with the **Prime Consultant**. Typical sub-consultants are structural, electrical, civil, and mechanical engineers; interior designers; landscape architects; acousticians, and telecommunications specialists.

Substantial Completion - The legal definition may vary from state to state, but the general concept from the **AIA** is that substantial completion is the stage in the construction of the project when it, or some designated portion thereof, is sufficiently complete in accordance with the **Contract Documents** for the **Owner** to occupy or utilize the facility as intended.

TANSTAAFL - There ain't no such thing as a free lunch.

Testing and Inspection - Part of the **Basic Services** provided by an **A/E**. It involves visits by an **A/E** to the construction site to verify compliance with material specifications and design intent. See also **Material Testing**.

UBC - The abbreviation for **Uniform Building Code**.

Uniform Building Code (1) - The model code of building and construction standards published by the International Conference of Building Officials. The UBC is adopted and enforced by most municipalities west of the Mississippi.

Users - The people who actually occupy and use a building. They are not necessarily synonymous with the "Owner," "agency," or institution. A failure to address the users' needs and desires will ensure an unsuccessful project, regardless of the "Owner's" intent or opinion.

Utility Infrastructure - The network of utility systems that support any building project, including power, water, sewer, chilled water, telecommunications, steam, etc. If the necessary utility infrastructure is not in place when a building is completed, the facility can't be "plugged in and turned on."

Value Engineering (1) - A process that identifies and assigns value to the various functions of a product or facility and then seeks a final design that maximizes functional value and reliability while minimizing cost. Also known as "VE." While value engineering should occur throughout the course of design, it most often is used toward the end of the process in order to reconcile a construction budget that is out of balance. Specialists in Value Engineering are also called "hatchet men" or "hackmeisters," although never to their face.

GLOSSARY RESOURCES:

(1) Facilities Planning Handbook, 3rd Edition, Edited by Lee Ingalls, Barbara Bruxvoort, and Jason Mihos; Published by Facilities Planning News, 1995.

(2) *Professional Liability in the Construction Process*, by Thomas L. Vance and Jack Doran; Published by DPIC Companies, 1998.

(3) *Architectural Programming*, by Donna P. Duerk; Published by Van Nostrand Reinhold, 1993.

(4) *Design Process*, by Sam F. Miller, AIA; Published by Van Nostrand Reinhold, 1995.

(5) *Architectural Programming*, by Robert Kumlin; Published by McGraw-Hill, 1995.

(6) *Problem Seeking*, 3rd Edition, by William Pena; Published by AIA Press, 1987.

(7) *The Architect's Studio Companion*, by Edward Allen and Joseph Iano; Published by John Wiley & Sons, 1995.

(8) *Major Projects Predesign Manual*, Published by the Washington State Office of Financial Management, 1994

(9) *Facilities Planning*, by Roger L. Brauer; Published by the American Management Association, 1986

Appendix A
Understanding Design Documents

Like any other field, architecture has its own terminology. Each kind of drawing is part of the field's visual vocabulary and uses its own perspective:

- Plan Drawings
- Section Drawings
- Elevation Drawings
- Paraline Drawings (also called Isometric or Axonometric Drawings)
- Perspective Drawings

Figure A-1.

Plan Drawings

A plan drawing is a two-dimensional representation of a three-dimensional reality, like looking down at an apple on a plate. (See Figure A-1) You see the building, a parking lot and landscaping surrounding it, and beyond them the property lines.

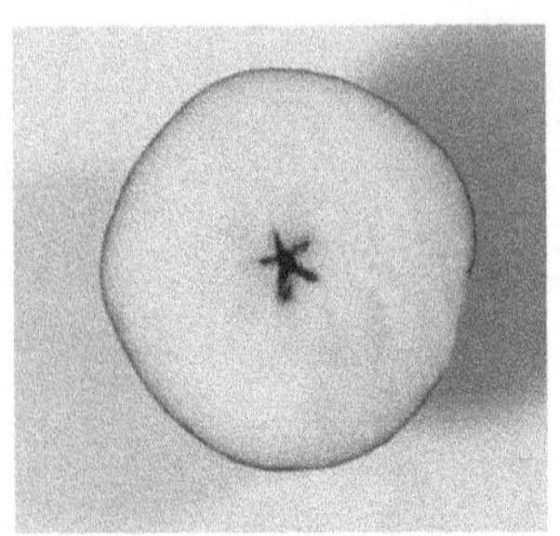

Figure A-2.

If you enlarge your view of the apple and expose its interior by slicing through it parallel to the table, you see this. (See Figure A-2).

A floor plan is essentially the same: a slice through the building, parallel to the ground, usually at an elevation of about four feet, or windowsill height. (See Figure A-3)

A plan view shows horizontal and spatial relationships. It does not show heights or the three-dimensional volume of a space very well. To illustrate vertical and spatial relationships, a designer uses section and elevation drawings.

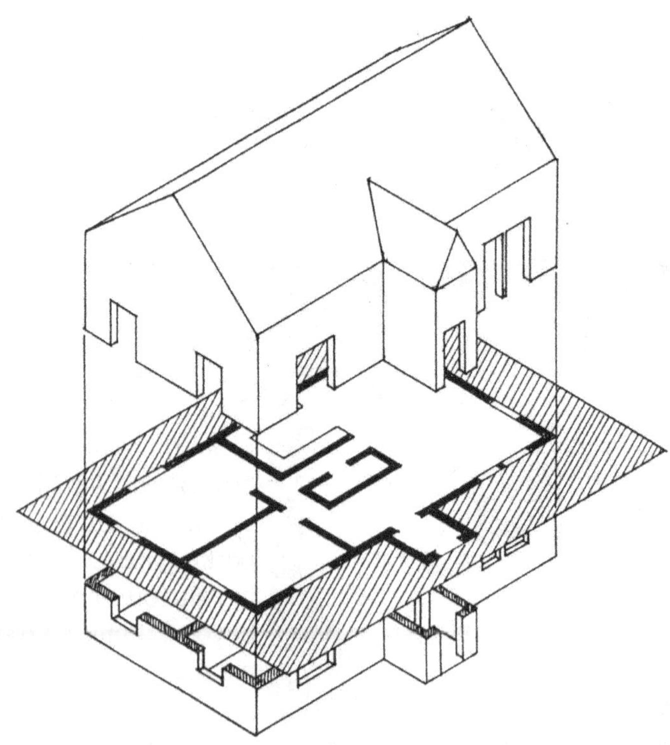

Figure A-3. Floor Plan

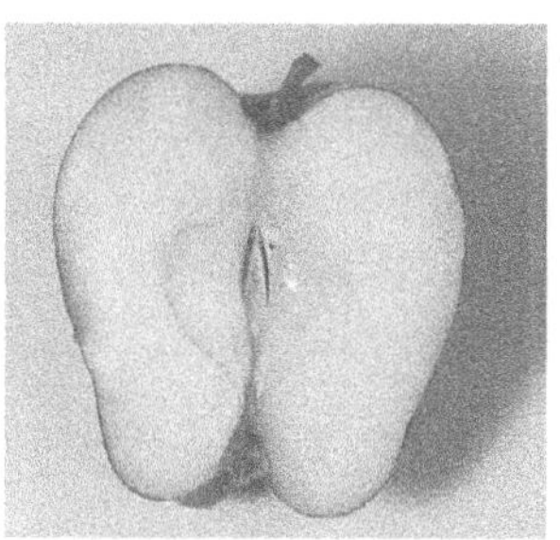

Figure A-4.

Section Drawings

If you slice the apple vertically, at a 90-degree angle to the table, you get a section view (See Figure A-4) that shows the profile of the apple: bottom, sides, and top. Most importantly, the section drawing shows the vertical relationships on the interior of the apple. Sections drawn at different points on the apple would show different interior elements.

A section drawing of a building shows the vertical relationships and vertical volumes that cannot be illustrated in a plan drawing, as though a giant knife sliced through the building from top to bottom, revealing its insides. (See Figure A-5)

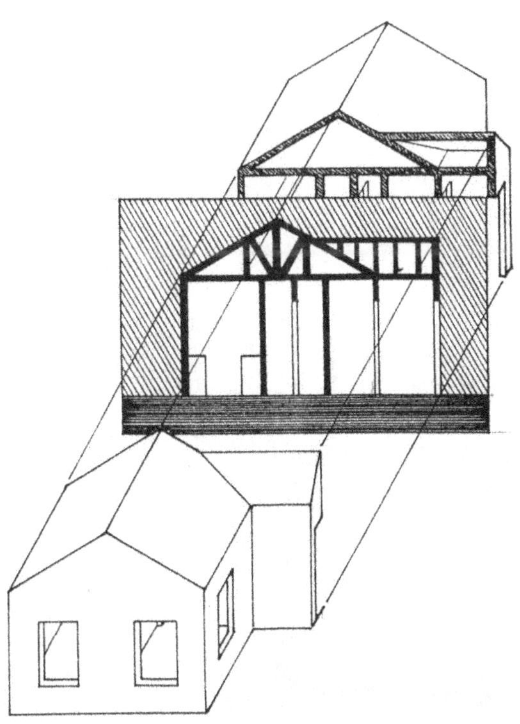

Figure A-5. Section View

Figure A-6.

Elevation Drawing

If you just look at the surface of our apple from the side, not from above (the plan view) or the interior (the section view), you would have an elevation view. (See Figure A-6)

The elevation drawing shows the face of the apple, or building. The architectural term for the face of the building is façade, from the Latin word for "face." (See Figure A-7)

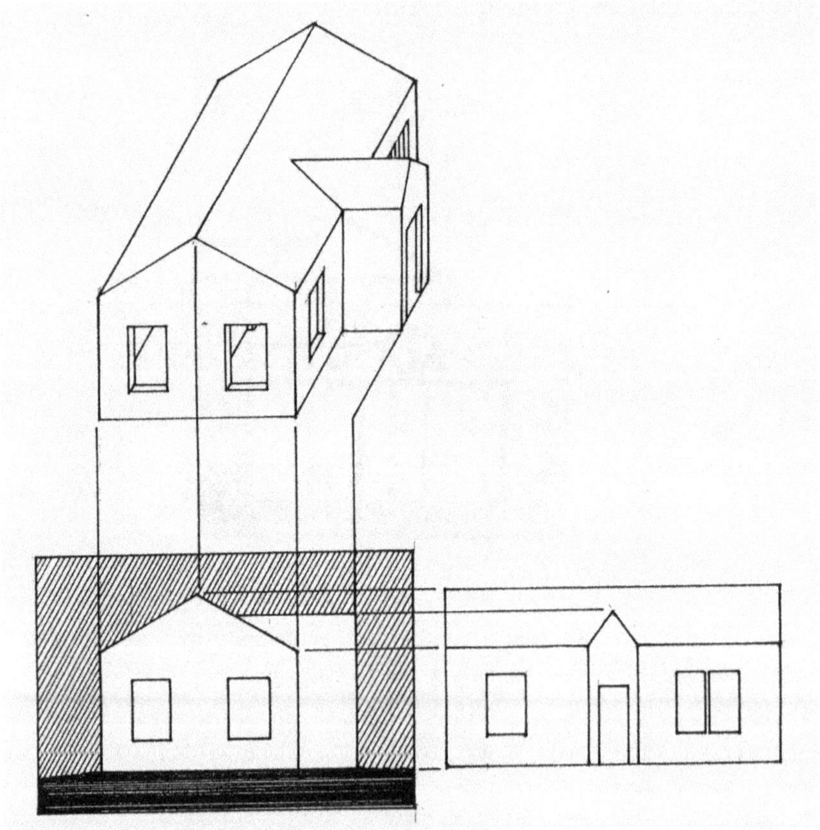

Figure A-7. Elevation View

Paraline Drawings

While the plan, section, and elevation drawings show the horizontal and vertical spatial relationships of the building, paraline drawings also show spatial volumes.

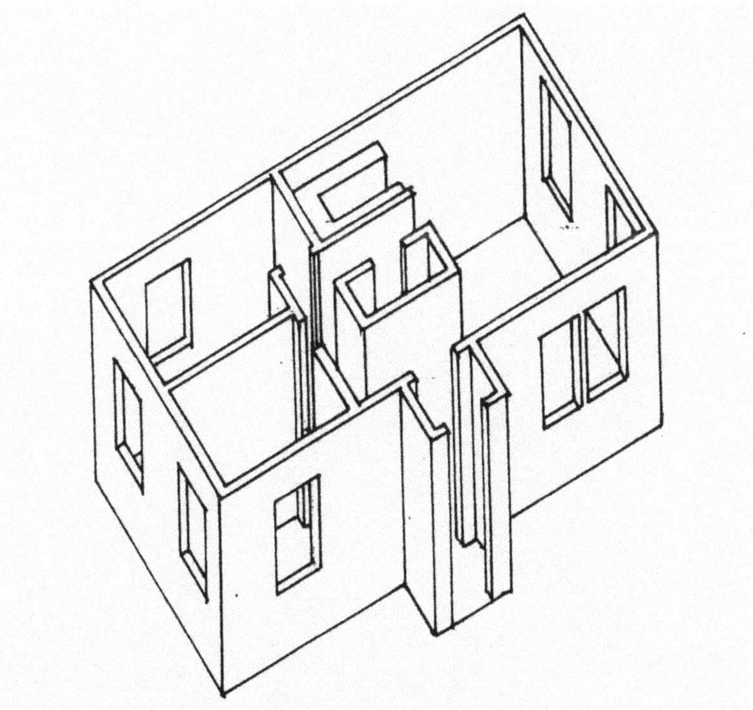

Figure A-8. Paraline Drawing

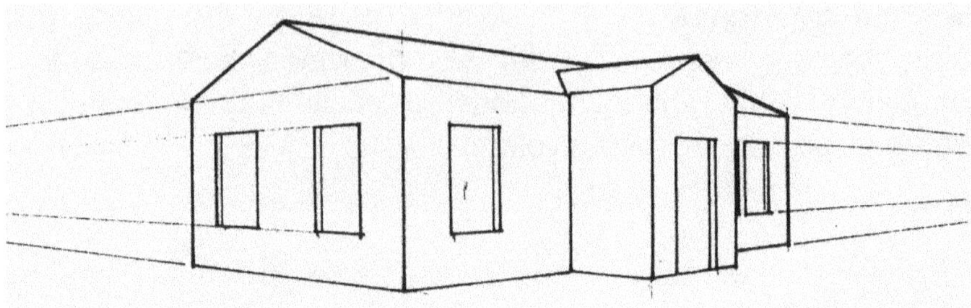

Figure A-9. Perspective Drawing

Perspective Drawings

Perspective drawings come the closest to depicting what we would see in reality. They are the easiest for the lay person to understand, which makes them very helpful for illustrative purposes. But they are not drawn to scale (at least not as accurately as other drawing forms are), so they can't be used for construction.(See Figure A-9)

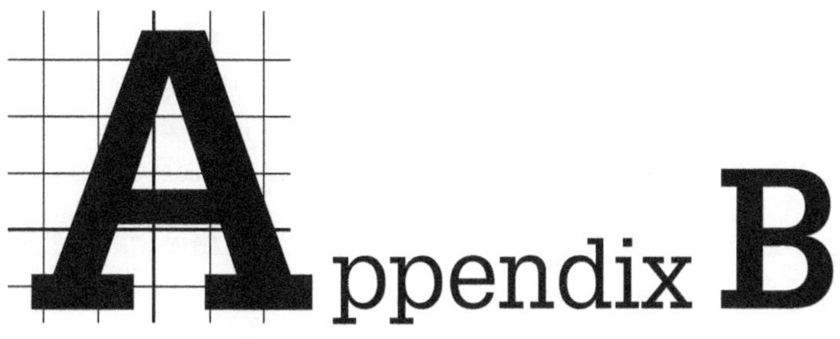

Appendix B
Annotated Bibliography and Recommended Reading List

Alexander, Christopher, *et al. A Pattern Language.* New York: Oxford University Press, 1977.

In my opinion, this is one of the best books ever written about architecture. Alexander has identified over 250 patterns of environmental design, ranging in scale from regions to how wide windowsills should be. Although theoretical, it is also eminently practical. Alexander won an AIA gold medal for this work, but when his criticisms of traditional architectural practice increased, the AIA considered revoking its award.

Allen, Edward, and Joseph Iano. *The Architect's Studio Companion: Rules of Thumb for Preliminary Design.* New York: John Wiley & Sons, 1995.

Useful for architects and those with some architectural training and experience, but readily accessible to all readers.

Allen, Edward. *How Buildings Work: The Natural Order of Architecture.* New York: Oxford University Press, 1995.

A lay person's guide to how architecture works and how building systems are best applied. A fun and interesting read.

Brand, Stewart. *How Buildings Learn: What Happens After They're Built.* New York: Viking, 1994.

Probably my second favorite book about architecture. Brand's approach is based on common sense, albeit often critical of architects. His views are especially germane to campus work, moreover, because many buildings on a campus are used over and over, experiencing a new life every few decades.

Brauer, Roger L. *Facilities Planning.* New York: American Management Association, 1986.

Cherry, Edith J. *Programming for Design: From Theory to Practice.* New York: John Wiley & Sons, 1999.

A valuable book on architectural programming.

Ching, Francis D.K. *Architecture: Form, Space and Order.* New York: Van Nostrand Reinhold, 1979.

A wonderful book that addresses architectural design from a visual point of view. Very useful overview, although not very technical.

Dober, Richard. *Campus Design.* Ann Arbor: Society for College and University Planning, 2003.

———. *Campus Planning.* Ann Arbor: Society for College and University Planning, 1996.

———. *Campus Architecture.* New York: McGraw-Hill, 1996.

Richard Dober has often been called the dean of campus planners. He has been practicing campus planning for 40 years and has been in the forefront of campus planning work for most of that time. His work has great utility for those actively engaged in the planning of campuses.

Duerk, Donna. *Architectural Programming: Information Management for Design.* New York: Van Nostrand Reinhold, 1993.

Another excellent work on programming.

Fink, Ira. Campus Planning and Facility Development: A Comprehensive Bibliography Fourth Edition. Berkley California: Ira Fink and Associates, Inc., 2002

Guckert, Donald, ed. *From Concept to Commissioning: Planning, Design, and Construction of Campus Facilities.* Alexandria: Association of Higher Education Facilities Officers, 2002.

A valuable collection of essays and articles that covers the range of capital project development from, well, "concept to commissioning." The chapters by Werner Sensbach (see below) on architectural design, and by Ksenia Merck and William Merck on pre-design planning, and by Blake Peck on delivery methods are especially useful.

Harris, Charles W., and Nicholas T. Dines. *Timesaver Standards for Landscape Architecture.* New York: McGraw-Hill, 1998.

A valuable resource for designers, especially those tasked with designing exterior environments on campus.

Hedman, Richard, and Andrew Jaszewski. *Fundamentals of Urban Design.* Chicago: American Planning Association, 1984.

Because campus planning has so many similarities to urban planning, Hedman and Jaszewski's book is very useful, even for non-architects.

Ingalls, Lee, Barbara Bruxvoort, and Jason Mihos, eds. *Facilities Planning Handbook, 3rd Edition.* Orinda: Tradeline, Inc., 1995.

Kenig, Michael. "Clarifying CM vs. CM At-Risk," *School Construction News,* January/February 2000, p. 12.

A simple and straigh forward description clarifying the distinctions between construction management and construction management at risk.

Kumlin, Robert R. *Architectural Programming: Creative Techniques for Design Professionals.* New York: McGraw Hill, 1995.

I have found Kumlin's work to be more practical and useful than either Duerk or Pena. Very handy for practitioners.

McClure, Ray. "Choosing Your Team," *American School and University*, November 1, 2002. Accessed August 6, 2004, online at http://asumag.com/mag/university_choosing_team/index.html

Miller, Sam F. *Design Process: A Primer for Architectural and Interior Designers.* New York: Van Nostrand Reinhold, 1995.

Pena, William, et al. *Problem Seeking: An Architectural Programming Primer.* Washington, D.C.: AIA Press, 1987.

Pena's work is considered the classic text in architectural programming. It was out of print for awhile, but the fourth edition was released by Wiley in 2001, so it is available again. Honestly, probably better suited for architects than non-architects, but it's clear enough to be readily understood by the non-architect.

Pollan, Michael. *A Place of My Own: The Education of an Amateur Builder.* New York: Random House, 1997.

See notes below on Rybczynski.

Rybczynski, Witold. *The Most Beautiful House in the World.* New York: Viking, 1989.

Both Pollan's book above and Ryczynski's book describe the design and construction process from the inside by individuals actively engaged in the process. Both books are very entertaining, readable, and instructional along the way (a rare and valuable combination). I include them here, not because they offer insight that couldn't be gained faster or easier elsewhere in this bibliography, but because many of the readers of this work will be academics and administrators who will find these two easier to relate to (they are about residential architecture) and far more entertaining than others on this list. What other justification does one need for a trip to the bookstore?

Sensbach, Wornor. "Restoring the Values of Campus Architecture," *Planning for Higher Education.* Vol. 20, Fall 1991, pp. 7–16.

One of the seminal articles in *Planning for Higher Education* regarding architectural design on campus. Sensbach provides guidelines that would benefit every campus if followed. This article can also be found in Guckert, above.

Turner, Paul Venable. *Campus: An American Planning Tradition.* Cambridge: The MIT Press, 1984.

Perhaps the best history of campus planning available. I have found it more useful than Dober's history of campus planning.

Vance, Thomas L., and Jack Doran. *Professional Liability in the Construction Process.* Monterey: DPIC Companies, 1998.

Very useful overview of the construction process and the liabilities facing architects, contractors, and owners. Especially useful for its descriptions of alternative construction delivery methods.

Van Yahres, Michel, and Syd Knight. "The Neglected Campus Landscape," *Planning for Higher Education.* Vol. 23, Summer 1995, pp. 20–26.

Another seminal article from *Planning for Higher Education*, but focused on the landscape architecture of campus.

Washington State Office of Financial Management. *Major Projects Predesign Manual*, 1994.

A very useful guide to the predesign process—also available online at www.ofm.wa.gov/budget/instructions/predesign/contents.htm

Yee, Roger. Educational Environments. New York: Visual Reference Publications Inc., 2002.

————. Educational Environments No. 2. New York: Visual Reference Publications Inc., 2005

Websites of Value

All of these websites were operational at the time of publication. Others can be found through simple Web searches.

The state of Washington's site for their Pre-design Process Manual. The glossary in pdf is also very valuable.
www.ofm.wa.gov/budget/instructions/predesign/contents.htm

Arizona State University's useful Capital Project Management glossary, which is also cited in the text, can be found at:
www.asu.edu/aad/manuals/cpm/cpm002.html

The following is a glossary that can also be accessed online:
www.pmforum.org/library/glossary/index.htm

Society for College and University Planning: www.scup.org

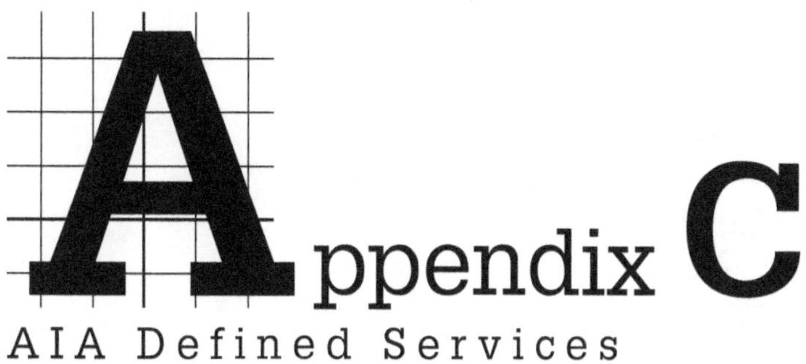

Appendix C

AIA Defined Services

"Schedule of Designated Services" excerpted from AIA form B163-1993 article 1.1. This article provides a worksheet to determine responsibility and method of payment for these and other services.

PROJECT ADMINISTRATION AND MANAGEMENT SERVICES

- Project Administration
- Disciplines Coordination/Document Checking
- Agency Consulting/Review/Approval
- Owner-Supplied Data Coordination
- Schedule Development/Monitoring of the Work
- Preliminary Estimate of Cost of the Work
- Presentation

DESIGN SERVICES

- Architectural Design/Documentation
- Structural Design/Documentation
- Mechanical Design/Documentation
- Electrical Design/Documentation
- Materials Research/Specifications

BIDDING OR NEGOTIATIONS SERVICES

- Bidding Materials
- Addenda
- Bidding/Negotiation
- Analysis of Alternates/Substitutions
- Special Bidding
- Bid Evaluation
- Contract Award

CONTRACT ADMINISTRATION SERVICES

- Submittal Services
- Observation Services
- Project Representation
- Testing and Inspection Administration
- Supplemental Documentation
- Quotation Requests/Change Orders
- Interpretations and Decisions
- Project Closeout

"Specifically Designated" services excerpted from AIA document B141-1997 section 2.8.3, based on the phases of a project as defined in this book.

THE PRE-DESIGN PLANNING PROCESS (FROM CHAPTER 1)

- Programming
- Existing Facilities Surveys
- Economic Feasibility Studies
- Site Analysis and Selection

THE DESIGN PROCESS (FROM CHAPTER 2)

- Space Schematics/Flow Diagrams
- Environmental Studies and Reports
- Geotechnical Engineering
- Land Survey Services
- Civil Design
- Landscape Design
- Interior Design

CONSTRUCTION ADMINISTRATION (FROM CHAPTER 3)

- Value Analysis
- Detailed Cost Estimating
- Construction Management
- On-Site Project Representation
- Start-Up Assistance
- Record Drawings
- Post-Contract Evaluation
- Tenant-Related Services

NOTES

NOTES

NOTES

NOTES

NOTES

NOTES

NOTES

NOTES

NOTES

www.ingramcontent.com/pod-product-compliance
Lightning Source LLC
Chambersburg PA
CBHW020707270326
41928CB00005B/312

* 9 7 8 1 9 3 7 7 2 4 5 9 7 *